AF631399

Methods of Social Work

METHODS OF SOCIAL WORK

A.K. Patel
M.V. Dubey

CRESCENT
PUBLISHING CORPORATION

[The responsibility for the facts stated, conclusions reached and plagiarism, if any, in this book is entirely that of the Author. And the Publisher bears no responsibility for them, whatsoever.]

Methods of Social Work

© Reserved

First Published : 2010

ISBN 978-81-8342-165-2

Published by :

CRESCENT PUBLISHING CORPORATION
4831/24, Prahlad Street,
Ansari Road, Darya Ganj,
New Delhi - 110002
Ph. : 23272541, 23257835
Fax : 91- 011- 23257835
e-mail : campusbooks@hotmail.com
commonwealth_pub@yahoo.com

Laser Typesetting by :
Anupama Computers
Delhi

Printed at :
Roshan Offset Printers
Delhi

Preface

Social work as a defined pursuit and profession began in the 19th century. This was in response to societal problems that resulted from the Industrial Revolution and an increased interest in applying scientific theory to various aspects of study. During the 20th century, the profession began to rely more on research and evidence- based practice as it attempted to improve its professionalism. Today social workers are employed in a myriad of pursuits and settings. They have organised themselves into local, national and international professional bodies to further the aims of the profession.

Social work bases its methodology on a systematic body of evidence-based knowledge derived from research and practice evaluation, including local and indigenous knowledge specific to its context. It recognises the complexity of interactions between human beings and their environment, and the capacity of people both to be affected by and to alter the multiple influences upon them including bio-psychosocial factors. The social work profession draws on theories of human development and social systems to analyse complex situations and to facilitate individual, organisational and social changes.

This book presents a comprehensive coverage of all important methods of social work. It provides readers an opportunity to develop knowledge ot the principles, values and methods of social work.

A.K. Patel
M.V. Dubey

Contents

Contents

1

Development of Social Work

Social work is a necessary component of international development. Social workers are trained to work with various stakeholders at community, national and international levels. Social workers are already engaged in a number of professional positions in the field of international development and are making meaningful contributions.

Social workers can ensure the "human aspect" is incorporated into international development efforts. Social work focuses on the process, the people, and the environment in the international development process which affects directly and indirectly on the well-being of all people who are involved. Social workers provide a "continuity of development" which is often lacking in international development efforts. Social workers provide a bridge between the development donor and the in-country beneficiaries and ought to be considered as an integral part of donor funding.

Ensuring that forms of practice are developed that pay full attention to its history and potential might form a useful corrective to the overwhelmingly 'administrative' nature of much contemporary social work. For example , in Jordan, there are different ways of interpreting the growth and development of social work as an organised activity. The first of these is the focus on *individual casework,* which originated in the work of the Charity Organisation Society (COS). The second is the role of social work in *social administration,* particularly (although not exclusively) involving various forms of relief from poverty. Although much of this originated from the Poor Law, it was also promoted in some of the work of the COS. The third is the focus on *social action,* which has been particularly identified with the growth of the Settlement Movement, both in Britain and the United States.

Individual Casework

Most historical accounts identify the COS as the initiator of the social theory that led to the formation of the occupation of social work. A particular element of the work of the COS was its focus on individual casework. One of the key contributions of the COS to social work was its clear – if perhaps partial and misguided – view of the cause of many social problems in Victorian Britain.

London, as graphically portrayed by Bosanquet, was seen as beset by a 'mass of chronic pauperism, beggary and crime', behind which lay 'an appalling amount of genuine misfortune'. In the view of the COS, existing services for the relief of poverty actually made matters worse, due to the inadequacy of the Poor Law combined with the counterproductive impact of the vast growth of charitable organisations. In the view of the COS, this combination stripped people of the will to fight against the circumstances in which they found themselves; by not making any distinction between those who did and did not merit support, it was held that the system in effect encouraged all people to throw themselves onto the combined ministrations of the Poor Law and charity rather than maintain their independence. The COS maintained that this weakened the family and hence had a profoundly negative impact on society at large.

To put their social theory into effect, the COS established systems and structures that enabled action in accordance with its principles. First and foremost, it insisted on proper coordination of charitable endeavour to avoid overlap and competition between organisations. To support this, an understanding was reached about the respective roles and purposes of the two arms of welfare, charity and the Poor Law. Charity was to be the first port of call for people in need, with the Poor Law and its institutions functioning as a general safety net beneath the charitable institutions. The next priority for the COS was to establish an organisational structure and a system to assist people who appeared to have some level of need.

While the COS did not originally intend to provide charity directly, but rather to coordinate the charitable provision of other organisations, District Committees of the COS soon became established to provide relief on their own account. The critical task was to oversee a process whereby a judgement could be made concerning the eligibility of applicants for support. This was accomplished by judging whether an applicant was considered to be 'deserving' or 'undeserving' of assistance. Even though the terminology used by the COS changed in later years, a moral dimension is clearly evident; this has had a continued impact on social work. It is in this process of investigation where the roots of social work practice can be clearly divined. If charity was to be properly directed, there needed to be a full, 'scientifically' organised examination of the circumstances of individuals and families who presented for a service. The basic techniques of 'casework' that the COS instigated have continued applicability.

For example, judgements had to be based on a detailed assessment of the applicant's circumstances, requiring home visits. The COS termed this 'taking down the case', a process that is clearly analogous to the preparation of assessments in contemporary practice. The COS issued guidance about how the process of 'taking down the case' should be organised; again, this role is broadly analogous to the guidance routinely issued by governments and employers to assist organisations and managers come to grips with changes in policy and practice. Following the assessment, a judgement was then to be made concerning an individual's eligibility to receive a service, which has its exact parallel in the existence of defined 'eligibility criteria' in current practice.

If services were to be provided, they could be of many different types, as is evident in the case histories that the COS cited in support of their work. The COS did not simply dispense financial charity, but also sought to find creative ways of maintaining and enhancing people's independence as such approaches were more in line with their governing philosophy. Although there was considerable variability between District Committees in terms of the number of people served and the quality of the investigations undertaken, the number of cases which the COS investigated was surprising to many, indicating that the organisation was uncovering a large amount of unmet need within society. However, its general approach was not popular, as is evident from the defensive tone throughout Bosanquet's history. While the COS took pride in the efficiency of its system, for many others it appeared harsh in the extreme. In addition, the COS was markedly hostile to other organisations involved in the provision of charity, as well as to other perceptions of the causes of poverty. It was apparently difficult to criticise the work of the COS – even in relatively mild terms – without provoking an antagonistic response; for example, the differences of view between the COS and Canon Barnett were addressed in a peculiarly arrogant and defensive manner.

In addition, the success of the COS in fulfilling its mission was also called into question, despite the robust way in which it sought to protect its position. Throughout its period of peak influence – up to the outbreak of the First World War in 1914– it was never able to escape from a paradox that it had itself created: 'The fact remained that the "unassisted" might be those who most needed help but least deserved it . . . while those helped, the respectable and provident, ought least to have needed help'. In addition, it was claimed that the perceived harshness of the COS approach actually promoted rather than curbed 'unscientific' charitable activity. It was also argued that the COS had not actually managed to classify the deserving and undeserving poor accurately, and that the charity that was dispensed was quite inadequate to combat need. As Webb concluded:

'the administration of the Poor Law . . . supplemented by charitable assistance according to the tenets of the C.O.S. . . . had next to no effect either on the poverty or on the misery of the poor'. These were powerful criticisms, which the COS struggled to combat successfully. In addition, the tide of opinion was shifting against the belief that the relief of poverty and distress was primarily an individual responsibility. In British society, following the cataclysm of the First World War, there was a much stronger level of acceptance that the provision of welfare was a matter for the state as much as the individual and the family. However, the influence of the COS on the development of social work was vast; in fact, it effectively created the occupation of social work, as well as defining many of its core tasks.

The COS also recognised that effective work required a level of training of those people undertaking it. Indeed, one of its most significant legacies to social work was the development of systematic programmes of education and training for the role of the social worker. With a diminution of the influence of the COS, a separation therefore appeared between the practice of individual casework and the social theory from which it originated. This was certainly a difficult time for social work in Britain, as it sought to establish a role and function that was separate from the specific ideas of the COS. One of the effects of the separation of social work methods from a broader social theory was a fragmentation in the occupational processes that sustained it.

For example, different branches of social work – psychiatric social workers, hospital almoners, etc. – operated separate systems of education and training, and in effect created parallel routes into the occupation. The search for an alternative rationale for social work was a preoccupation for much of the next part of its existence. The importation of a collection of ideas from the USA was to have a particular importance in this respect. The first of these was the detailed codification of the process of 'social diagnosis' undertaken by Mary Richmond, which was an early attempt to establish a common base for all social work practice. Richmond asserted that: 'in essentials, the methods and aims of social case work were or should be the same in every type of service'.

Central to this was the act of assessing needs, which should be based on a systematic process of gathering 'social evidence' from a range of sources – the individual, family members, and outside sources such as schools, doctors, employers, etc. The key contribution of Richmond to the development of social work was in the detailed, 'scientific' organisation of data that she propounded, which represented a major step forward along the path first outlined by the COS. The second major import stemmed from the popularity of psychologicallybased theories in American social work from the 1920s onwards.

Cormack and McDougall suggested that the introduction of treatment methods deriving from related disciplines did little to suggest that a social worker possessed unique expertise and was hence worthy of professional status; it appeared that a social worker was doing nothing that could not equally well be accomplished by many other occupations – and even mature people of good sense lacking any qualification at all. Nevertheless, the adoption of psychologically-oriented insights increased the focus of social work on the workings of the mind, as is apparent from the content of one of the most significant post-war textbooks on social casework in Britain.

The attraction of 'universal applicability' for social work approaches was obvious, particularly given the occupation's fragmentation in the first half of the twentieth century. A focus on social casework informed by psychological theories offered the prospect of unifying these disparate elements. Indeed, the first 'generic' training course for social workers was established for precisely this purpose. The increased confidence that this gave to the social work world should not be underestimated – it suffuses all the contributions to Morris' seminal text.

For example, Younghusband is somewhat patronising to the pioneers of social work practice who managed to operate without the knowledge of 'unconscious motivations, behaviour patterns, the transference situation, client–worker relationships, social maladjustment, obsessional behaviour, the need to express feelings of guilt and aggression, reactions to deprivations in childhood' that were the stock in trade of the 'modern' practitioner. She is clear that social work practice had developed for the better as a result of the increased knowledge that social workers had of the innermost workings of people. In addition, she is in little doubt of the greater levels of skill and knowledge that could be required of the social worker. The scope of the social work task, as Younghusband defined it, was greatly increased – indeed, it was ambitiously framed. However, there was an element of unreality in her description: only a small minority of people could receive the sort of service she identified. It was difficult for social workers in statutory agencies to accommodate these requirements into their daily work, as Rodgers and Stevenson made clear.

Even in voluntary organisations, the ideals of individual casework were difficult to put into practice. However, the way in which the social work task was theorised represented an elaborate updating of its key elements. However, it was this very ambition that caused one of the most notable attacks on the developing occupation of social work. In her book *Social Science and Social Pathology* Barbara Wootton excoriated what she saw as social work's obsession with methods drawn from psychiatry and psychology. The essence of her critique was that the fascination with psychology and psychiatry created a 'fantastically pretentious façade' for the occupation, resulting from 'a tendency to emphasise certain aspects of social work, while playing down others that are potentially at least as valuable'. She identified the rhetoric that accompanied descriptions of social work practice as particularly worrying, and mocked the idea that social work could actually achieve the sorts of change its advocates appeared to propose. Her preferred remedy was that social work should rediscover a more modest focus on helping people by acting as what she termed a 'middleman': mobilising, organising and coordinating the services of a huge range of other professional colleagues, and by guiding people through the mass of legislation and policy that could affect them. In this way, Wootton suggested that the social worker could once again be essential to the effective functioning of the welfare state.

While this was a witty and stimulating critique, Wootton's analysis did not engage fully with the reality that confronted social workers. Her conception of the limited role of social work offered little that could assist, for example, an abused child, a person with a mental health problem, or people who had experienced bereavement, all of whom would require an approach that was more in line with that suggested by the advocates of individual casework. In addition, Wootton's perception of the role of social work did not accord with the reality of what practitioners actually did – vividly conveyed by Rodgers and Stevenson – but related more closely to the rhetoric of those whose role it was to promote the development of social work.

With the benefit of hindsight, the 1950s represented the period where individual casework was most highly prized within social work. However, as we have seen, one key problem with this formulation was that it did not equate to much of the actual practice of people employed as social workers, particularly those working within statutory settings. For such people, there remained an emphasis on the efficient administration of relief; this will be the focus of the next section. In addition, it moved the occupation a long way from its origins as a social movement; the idea that social work can be seen as a movement interested in securing social change is the focus of the section after that. In terms of work with older people it had relatively little impact; the role of social worker has always had more of an element of administrative requirements.

Social Work as Social Administration

As various commentators have noted social work has its earliest roots – even pre-dating the formation of the COS – in the work of the Poor Law relieving officers, whose duty was to administer the system that had first been created through the Poor Law Act of 1601. The importance of their role was given additional stimulus by the Poor Law Amendment Act of 1834, which emphasised the element of deterrence through the formal introduction of the concept of 'less eligibility'. This meant that the conditions of relief would consciously be made no better than was available to the lowest paid worker, in order not to make such relief more attractive to those who might be eligible for it and hence discourage their desire to engage in productive labour. The Poor Law was administered on a local level by Boards of Guardians, which gave rise to considerable variation in the way in which it was managed across the country.

All Boards of Guardians required some basis of making judgements about the eligibility of applicants to forms of relief, which were generally financial. Relieving officers were widely employed to accomplish this end in the early years of the nineteenth century. By contrast with the COS or the Settlement Movement it was not generally argued that these officers required a formal period of education and training to accomplish their tasks: as a result their quality was variable. Although a National Poor Law Officers' Association was formed in 1884, seeking to improve the status and quality of the occupation through better professional training, this had little effect on the low public esteem in which it was held.

However, the 1929 Local Government Act did manage to achieve some degree of change for this group of staff, as the responsibility for managing the Poor Law transferred to the direct control of local government, with the relieving officers redesignated as public assistance officers. In their location, as well as in some of their work, the influence of these staff on the development of social work is considerable. Elements of social administration were also contained in the role of workers within the COS. For example, although much assistance was other than financial, direct financial support was provided in some instances.

The rhetoric of casework most affected social work in the 1950s it was accepted that the social worker needed to have a good understanding of the range and scope of resources that could be made available to an individual or family. Indeed, the conception that the social work role was, at least in part, concerned with humanising the administration of social services was well accepted. This general perception lasted through reorganisation in the early 1970s, which coincided with a rapid increase in the numbers of qualified social workers. In reality, irrespective of the rhetoric of individual casework (or, indeed, the rhetoric of the later radical social work) much of the practice of social workers was concerned with responding to the minutiae of people's lives in a practical and pragmatic fashion.

Throughout this period, there is little doubt that the administrative elements of the social work role far outweighed the elements that derived from casework, particularly in respect of older people. It was in recognition of this that very little practice with older people was actually carried out by qualified staff until the passage of the National Health Service and Community Care Act 1990. Even though this legislation increased the numbers of qualified staff employed to work with older people, care management – the dominant form of social work practice with older people – particularly emphasised the administrative role of the practitioner.

The social work role was increasingly restricted to the act of assessment, leading to the establishment of care packages and the rapid closure of the 'case'. Arguably, these trends have made social work with older people into a particularly dispiriting enterprise for many practitioners. Although the 'administrative' elements of social work have a long history, it is the development of 'casework' that has been more frequently cited as the main contributor to the development of the occupation of social work. However, the origins of social work in social administration are apparent, and this focus for practice remains evident.

Social Action: The Settlement Movement

The earliest example of social work as a form of collective social action in Britain can be found in the work of the Settlement Movement, established by Canon Barnett in the 1880s. The Settlement Movement was underpinned by a number of beliefs that it shared with the COS. Both were based on similar moral principles, even though different forms of practice stemmed from these principles; a belief in the value of education and example underpinned the values of both. In addition, both accepted that financial assistance was insufficient to combat problems within communities and individuals. Similarly, both had their origins in the sense of obligation of the more privileged to those less fortunate than themselves, and shared a strong belief in the purpose and value of education, establishing training courses in conjunction with universities.

Gilchrist and Jeffs have indicated that the movement was based on three linked ideas:

- The need to develop scientific research on the causes and effects of poverty.
- That the 'settlers' could help to broaden the lives and horizons of people and communities through education.
- That they could also enhance leadership within local communities.

As this outline indicates, its practice differed from the work of the COS. For example, it was not predicated on resolving immediate individual needs, but rather sought to work through the community and the group to improve general social conditions. Critically, the vision of Canon Barnett was different from that of the COS on one key point, relating to the social theory that underpinned the Settlement Movement.

Barnett came to believe that the root causes of poverty and distress could be located in social structures more than in the defects of individual character; he termed the action that followed this diagnosis 'practical socialism'. His vision was that people of education – the movement attracted women as well as men – could establish a relationship with people of a different class to their mutual benefit. The residence requirement for 'settlers'was critical for this; while most worked outside the community for their paid employment, they spent other time undertaking forms of community service and development.

To the modern reader, there seems at least as much unifying as dividing the COS and the Settlement Movement – and some early pioneers like Octavia Hill supported both– but the division was deeply felt by the COS at least. The explanation for this can be located in the clarity of the COS vision: if the analysis on which it was based was accurate, then only one possible set of responses could logically follow. Any divergence from this path was treated almost as apostasy.

Although the Settlement Movement initially expanded quite quickly in Britain –and with even more speed in the USA – its growth did not outlive the main establishing pioneers. By 1914 there were 46 settlements; these were a mixture of women-only, men-only and mixed establishments. However, as the education and training of 'settlers' developed, the pioneers tended to be replaced by 'professionals', who saw their role as consolidating the innovations that they inherited, rather than devising new ones. As a result, as Seed pointed out, the nature of the movement gradually changed, losing much of its radical edge.

With the decline in significance of the Settlement Movement paralleled by the advance of individual casework, there was little connection in social work practice in the middle years of the twentieth century to the strand of social action and community development that had motivated Canon Barnett and his followers. Indeed, the 1950s and early part of the 1960s represented the almost total eclipse of collective action as part of social work. However, a coherent critique of the contemporary state of social work was mounted from the late 1960s onwards, focusing on the failures of a practice that 'pathologised' the individual while ignoring the material and social causes of poverty and disadvantage. The establishment of the radical journal *Case Con* in 1970 was a key moment in this process, providing a focal point for an alternative conception of the potential of social work.

This was more fully articulated in a variety of texts in the late 1970s and early 1980s, of which Bailey and Brake, Jones and Simpkin are a representative sample from the UK. They are part of a movement that became known as 'radical social work' after the title of Bailey and

Brake's important text. Although there were differences amongst the proponents of radical social work, particularly in the way in which they addressed issues of inequality that were other than class-based, they shared an understanding of the causes of human problems that sought to shift the focus of social work intervention in a profound way, moving away from an individual to a collective response to problems.

While influential within the academy and within certain areas of practice, ultimately radical social work as a 'movement' foundered on some barely recognised contradictions. For example, while its analysis of social problems was a necessary corrective to the highly individualised understandings within 'casework', it was much less effective in guiding social workers towards alternative models of practice. As Cohen observed, the emphasis on structural causes of disadvantage did not necessarily enable individuals to address the specific problems that they encountered. In addition, the radical social work agenda appeared to assume that social workers had more capacity to challenge and change policy than was realistic, given their occupational location.

Certainly, employers did not expect their staff to foment revolution, despite the apparent inducement so to do within some radical social work material! This was particularly true from the 1980s onwards, a difficult period for the development of more progressive forms of social work. Finally, the early analyses of the radical social work movement were heavily class-based, with relatively little attention devoted to issues of race, gender, disability, sexuality, etc. This meant that it did not connect sufficiently well with groups of people – practitioners and service users alike – who could have been allies. It is perhaps significant that the radical social work movement was relatively short-lived, failing to surmount either the challenges provided by the changed social and political climate of the 1980s or the different sorts of critique mounted by Black people, women and disabled people. It had less impact on social work than it had intended, but the sorts of analysis that it engendered have proved to have a continuing influence. Its impact on social work with older people was particularly limited. As an attempt to re-focus social work onto its potential to operate as a social movement it was only partly successful, but it certainly helped to draw attention to various issues – the impact of poverty, the potential of community – that had been long neglected.

Issues in Contemporary Social Work

The political critique of social work that had particular force from the 1960s on was from the 'radical social work' movement, the outline of which was sketched in the previous section. It rejected what it saw as the pathologising elements of individual casework, notably the common assumption that poverty was the result of personal failure rather than economic forces. It pressed for the establishment of a form of practice that re-engaged with the economic basis of disadvantage, drawing on ideas of community development and social action that are traceable to the Settlement Movement.

Radical social work largely rejected the notion of individual casework, believing that this distracted from the central mission of social work, which it saw as combating poverty and disadvantage. The critique from the right was of a different order, focusing on the fundamental ineffectiveness of social work. Brewer and Lait contended that social work was imprecisely defined, encompassing too broad a range of roles and functions. They argued that it should be much more narrowly focused and defined, and followed Wootton in questioning the essence of social work's claims for professional status, believing that social workers were 'valued but *essentially subordinate* employees of the traditional health and welfare agencies', whose role was basically to carry out the practical work of such agencies. Brewer and Lait further suggested that the diffuse, over-ambitious and ill-defined aims of social services departments ensured the futility of much practice, and that the poor quality of the education and training offered to social workers further compounded the problems. Their conception of social work had the practitioner occupying a predominantly bureaucratic position, with 'professional' training replaced by a form of apprenticeship.

These criticisms of social work found a ready audience within certain sections of the media and politics, not to mention the medical profession. However, their analysis is contaminated by the prejudiced language in which it is conveyed, with constant disparaging barbs directed to all and sundry within social work and a dismissive tone towards all knowledge that is not based in hard, scientific certainty.

Critical areas of contention were laid out in two contrasting minority reports, one of which was largely the work of Roger Hadley, the other being solely the work of Robert Pinker. Hadley and colleagues advocated for the extension of the notion of community social work, the most controversial of the recommendations of the main report. They argued that the central role of social work should be to support informal caring networks; in order to do this, they suggested that a community-oriented approach had to be developed. In their view, such an orientation required four conditions to be met:

— *Localisation*: 'statutory services must be local enough to operate at street and village level'.

— *Integration*: three kinds of integration were suggested – integration within each social services department, integration between the department and other service-providing agencies, and integration between the department and social networks.

— *Wider roles*: to accomplish this fundamental shift, staff roles had to be defined much less narrowly than before.

— *Greater autonomy*: 'local social services teams will need a larger measure of discretion to develop these approaches than they have been formally accorded'.

There had been a number of projects that had explored this sort of practice, and the alternative view adopted by Hadley and colleagues was firmly in this tradition. However, this conception of the social work role did not fit comfortably with the increasingly coercive nature of social workers' activities, particularly in respect of child protection. Pinker took a diametrically opposite position, contending that social workers had no mandate for the sorts of activity that could be grouped under the banners either of 'community social work' or 'neighbourhood social work'. He argued that both the majority report and the minority appendix of Hadley and colleagues were based on fundamentally flawed premises.

The concept of 'community' on which they founded their analysis was not clearly defined, there were fatal ambiguities in the concepts of accountability that were deployed, and unresolved tensions between the principles of 'specialism' and 'genericism' within social work practice. By contrast, Pinker recommended that social work would be more securely defined in a manner that was limited by its statutory remit.

In the 1980s there were challenges to social work from groups – women, Black people, service user groups, the advocacy movement, etc. – who had been subject to the services of social workers. These challenges have been usefully summarised by Taylor, who argued that the groups share common purposes, despite their obvious differences, in their focus on issues such as diversity, universalism, power and rights. The tests that these movements have posed for social work served to expose fundamental elements of the occupation's self-image.

- A key underlying theme is that their criticisms highlight the fact that social work has often failed to live up to its more lofty ideals. Given that an important principle of social work has always been its ability to respond positively to the most disadvantaged sections of society, this condemnation highlights a dismal failure within the occupation.
- The groups have also highlighted social workers' inability to work effectively in practice with individual disabled people, black people, gays and lesbians, etc.

In combination, these concerns helped to create a climate of uncertainty and doubt within social work, attesting to the fact that it was an occupation in some disarray.

Working on the assumption that disputes about the nature of social work are really disputes about the nature and causes of, and solutions to, social problems, the different perspectives on social work therefore represent alternative views on the role that the occupation plays within society. In this respect Mullaly has differentiated between broadly 'conventional' and 'progressive' perspectives on the role and functions of social work. In the 'conventional' view – which he suggests is, and always has been, held by the majority of the profession – the structure of society is believed to be fundamentally sound.

The broad role of social work is therefore either to help people adjust to existing social structures, or to amend those structures in a limited way. In the minority 'progressive' view the purpose of social work is different, being primarily to contribute to a fundamental social transformation, on the basis that the problems of individuals are caused by inequitable social structures rather than individual inadequacy or weakness. In the foregoing debate about the origins of social work, the efficient administration of relief and most individual casework can be placed within the 'conventional' perspective.

Indeed, support for the *status quo* was a central part of the role of the COS. In addition, there is relatively little in the literature on individual casework that argues for a more radical social vision. By contrast, the Settlement Movement contained the seeds of a more critical perspective; it is therefore no surprise that many future socialist politicians – including the future Prime Minister Clement Attlee – were active in this movement in their youth. This critical perspective became more explicit in the radical social work movement.

An alternative way of conceptualising different perspectives on social work has been devised by Payne. He has suggested that three 'general perspectives' on social work can be identified: 'individualist-reformist', 'socialistcollectivist', and 'reflexive-therapeutic'. The discipline of social work is held to contain elements of these three perspectives, with one or another being influential at different times. For example, the reflexive-therapeutic perspective was particularly powerful in the USA in the early part of the twentieth century, being imported for British consumption in the years following the Second World War.

The socialist-collectivist perspective was especially prominent in the radical social work literature in Britain in the 1970s and early 1980s. By contrast, most social work in contemporary Britain is more within the individualist-reformist tradition, which has been influentially articulated by Martin Davies, who claimed that, 'although social workers have many roles . . . they are all subsumed under a general theory of *maintenance*'. That this has become the dominant perspective is far from being a matter of chance, as it accepts the basic structures of society and sets limits to the social work role that circumscribe its focus.

While these are helpful ways of conceptualising the place of social work, they do both over-simplify some of the inherent contradictions that characterise daily practice. To take Mullaly's split, even if a practitioner were to espouse a 'progressive' view of social work, s/he must necessarily frequently *act* in ways that support the framework of society: the legislative and statutory basis of social work requires no less. Similarly, it is at least conceptually possible for a social worker to practise in accordance with all of Payne's 'general perspectives' on social work at different times: they are not mutually exclusive.

In reality, the bulk of what a social worker actually does in practice with older people in Britain will fit within the individualist-reformist perspective, simply because the key statutory and policy requirements of the agencies within which most of them operate – carrying out community care assessments, arranging for safe and speedy hospital discharges, etc. – lend themselves to this orientation to social work. However, a social worker should not forget that there are other perspectives on which to draw. For example, s/he might recognise that an older person needs additional support to come to terms with loss and bereavement, or that a carer for a person with dementia has a particular need for counselling to come to terms with the changes that dementia engenders. Both examples are of work that fits within a more therapeutic tradition. Similarly, on different occasions a social worker might perceive the need for collective action, for example by supporting a group of carers to meet, or by enabling the formation of service user groups to argue for better services.

Social workers need to be capable of working in three different but complementary approaches:

— Working with individuals, in both problem-solving and therapeutic ways.

— Working as a go-between, ensuring that resources are mobilised to meet need, with particular stress on the tasks of liaison and coordination.

— Working with groups and communities, to construct creative and new types of response to problems, including the development of new services and resources.

This approach recognises that human problems are complex and that the ways of responding to them are manifold. An *individualist/therapeutic,* an *administrative* or a *collectivist* response may be indicated at different times; the practitioner has to retain the capacity to identify what approach is more likely to be effective, and at what time. In addition, and this is particularly true for practice with older people, the functions of agencies need to be constructed in ways that allow for this element of flexibility on the part of the social worker.

2

Importance of Social Work Interventions

It is impossible to separate the need for social work intervention from the role of social work. This is integral to deciding social work's contribution to tackling social and personal problems and promoting well-being. Claiming exclusive territory is not appropriate for social work because:

— the whole of the person's life situation and social context is its focus

— the implementation of its values and the process are what give social work its quality - 'there are no good outcomes without good processes'.

This creates difficulties for social work because professions usually define their territory through an exclusive claim to specific knowledge and skill. This lack of exclusive territory leads to the regular prediction of the demise of social work.

Social work's role is carried out through:

— direct practice, of various types and techniques, with individuals, families, groups and communities and with provider organisations

— the management and development of:
  - practice, including work based learning for students and staff
  - service provision, including commissioning
  - policy and strategy within, and outside the organisation
— working with a range of organisations to contribute to the promotion of social and personal well-being
— research and development.

The organisational context in which social workers operate is significant in determining:

— whether good practice is in spite of, or because of its support
— whether the management of practice is fit for purpose in a particular context
— the nature of the teams within which social workers are operating
— whether there is a learning environment that supports good practice so that social workers are confident about their knowledge and skills.

Knowledge and skill shifts occur over time

— particularly when there are significant changes in social policy
— both within and between professions and occupational groups
— because people using services build up their own expertise and this becomes incorporated into the knowledge used by professionals
— when new groupings of knowledge and skill emerge in response to new needs and policy directions
— as solutions become more standardised or there are technological developments skills move from professionals to members of the public.

Need for Social Work Intervention

Most social workers are currently expected to cover a huge span of approaches. This may not be appropriate in the future. Different strands can be identified, which, while not exclusive of each other, form the primary focus individual social workers' interventions. We have identified three:

Intervening between the State and the Citizen

This occurs when:

- national or local state funded assistance is required to remove blocks to the outcomes people using service prefer. Since social work services have never been universal, this function requires someone to assess eligibility in order to ration scarce resources. Determining eligibility is required whether the support/service is funded through national or local state or voluntary or business organisations.
- statutory intervention is triggered to keep the child, young person, adult or others safe from harm. Here the social worker assesses whether the risks are at or above the thresholds for statutory intervention. The circumstances in which this can happen are set out in statute, regulation, guidance and standards and moderated by the judicial system. It is an area where there is often conflict about the need for, the appropriateness of and adequacy of the intervention. Decisions are high risk and complex, often involving moral and ethical elements and human rights issues.

This is the predominant approach to social work based in local authorities. Its strength is that it combines a commitment to personalised support through accessing a wide range of support and balances the needs of the individual with those of others. There are five significant dangers:

- a limited range of social work skills is used. Social work becomes equated with assessment and determining eligibility to access scarce resources. Negotiation with people using services about what they want to achieve can be transformed into consultation, a lower level of power sharing
- social workers' capacity building through community development is minimised
- resources (time and expertise as well as money) are diverted towards children and families away from older people, disabled people and people with learning disabilities
- workers can become institutionalised and accept 'the way it is done here' uncritically, in effect abandoning professional judgement. When reinforced by a command and control management, they protect themselves against criticism by retreating into description rather than make professional judgements.
- statutory work operates a significant pull on resources to cover risks to the organisation as opposed to the citizen whether child or adult. Bureaucratisation of decision can means that it can take months before clearance is given for a foster child to stay overnight with friends, go on trips or have their ears pierced. This level of caution (which denies young people the 'normal life' they want and is expensive in organisational time) contrasts with the expectation that many young people will begin to live independently at 16 years old.

Maximise the Capacity of People Using Services

The objective is that individuals, as far as possible, are, or become, 'expert clients' or 'informed clients'. For children and young people the aim is:

- to achieve permanent and stable emotional and social relationships
- to assist them to cope with impediments, in their past or present, to minimise or remove their impact on life options
- to secure supplementary support for their educational, health, social and emotional development
- to move as smoothly as possible through the usual developmental and transition stages of growing up.

For adults it offers an opportunity to think through with a social worker the obstacles to their well-being, or to have a social care check, similar to a health check. Social work intervention enables citizens to think through how to build on their expertise and experience by:

- working with people to navigate through the maze of information, organisations and options so that they can create a personalised plan
- providing help lines and desks for individuals, community and user led groups, other professionals and organisations
- connecting people with similar experiences with each other and with user led organisations or community organisations
- providing information and contacts to build capacity
- providing therapeutic support
- challenging attitudes, behaviour and services that block people's capacity to take as much control over their lives as possible
- mediating between state organisations and citizens
- advocating directly or linking people to advocacy
- spotting and supporting effective innovations.

There is no reason that this form of intervention should not be a universal service on a similar basis to the General Practitioner. Such a development may require the separation of assessment from the provision of services. It would not promise unrealistic access to services, or create the expectation of statutory intervention except in clearly defined circumstances with high thresholds. Citizens who can afford to pay for services already access this support through independent social workers or counsellors, many of whom are social work qualified. There is no known research on the range of work undertaken by independent social workers, but anecdotal evidence indicates that such support is focused on:

For children

- managing transitions for children such as the ending of a family unit and reconstituting new family groups
- building confidence and self esteem
- survival strategies for children and young people bullied in school
- reaching decisions about whether to move to independent living
- coping with family conflicts
- coping with death, loss and change

For adults

- loss, separations and bereavements
- relationships with partners
- life options
- coping with trauma, such as sudden illness or impairment
- parenting problems and behavioural management

The strengths of this form of intervention are that:

- power is shared more equally and people retain control over their lives or specific areas of them
- the main resources are people's own expertise and experience, their capacity to learn, and the resources that exist in their social networks
- the individual has sought the intervention by the social worker.

The social worker's skills in forming and using relationships in problem solving, negotiation and conflict resolution are used within a social model. There is a high level of coherence between the value base of social work and the Codes of Practice for Social Care and the work.

The dangers are that social workers can become isolated from professional support or have to fit into a model of professional support that is not fit for purpose. A range of approaches will need to be developed in addition to the traditional social work supervision at fixed times, for example, 'hovering supervision' or supervision 'at the end of a phone' that gives rapid access to the worker.

Policies and Practices for Social and Personal Well-being

Although all social work requires the capacity to work with and through others, in this approach this is the social worker's primary role. The aim is to contribute to building the 'platforms' from which personalised services can be developed and through which citizens can promote their own well-being or manage long term conditions. Policy development roles could include promoting Direct Payments within health, education and housing. Elder-Woodward argues that the social workers' role in community development should include capacity building for user-led support systems as a way 'to empower people not only to control their own lives but to be in some way accountable to and for their own support systems'. The worker can be located in a wide variety of organisations in the statutory, voluntary or private sectors, in user-led organisations, community groups, schools, health, the police, businesses, local or national government. Skills include:

- the capacity to spot and manage conflicts
- working within different power structures
- negotiation within a framework of equality and empowerment
- navigation through the maze of organisations, programmes, initiatives, issues and options
- promoting social inclusion of marginalised groups in partnerships
- communicating how social care contributes to health, education, community capacity building, community safety, productivity
- building and maintaining networks or teams.

Strengths and Weaknesses of the Approach

The strengths are that the social work knowledge and expertise in promoting social inclusion is incorporated into new arenas. It provides a 'social well-being impact statement' as an integral part of social, economic and environmental change. The weaknesses are that the social worker can become isolated from professional support and developments, fail to identify where compromises have been made without considering the consequences or using evidence about the implications this may have in the short, medium and longer term.

Achievement of Well-being

An outcomes approach to need can be used in all these forms of intervention. In the vast majority of instances the obstacles to people achieving the outcomes they want are related to their economic poverty. The result of this is that they are likely:

- to be living in poor housing,
- to have lower educational attainment
- to have poorer health and for their children to have a higher incidence of accidents requiring hospital admission
- to have a lower life expectancy
- to be unemployed
- to have reduced chances of living in a decent and safe environment or access to leisure, recreation and transport.

Although poverty and its consequences affect the majority of people using services, the resources to address these issues are outwith the control of social work and care. For some people problems arise because of a combination of economic, relationship, health and emotional factors. Social work may be drawn on in any of these situations.

Social work is a collective activity because it works with and through other people, through partnership with other organisations. To be effective social work partnerships have to include people using services or at least their agreement to participate. Without this the task is limited to monitoring behaviour or activities.

Categories of Need for Social Work Intervention

There are three main categories where a need for social work intervention may arise. These are:

1. When people know they face obstacles to achieving the outcomes they want to achieve and seek intervention because:

- they, their families, their support networks or communities cannot overcome them, or
- the costs (physical, emotional, social and financial) to them are too high in the short, medium or longer term, or
- the resources needed are so specialised that they are only available through a social work, educational, medical or housing assessment.

2. When people do not seek, or necessarily welcome, intervention because they are not aware of ways of overcoming the obstacles they face, or lack the information, knowledge and/skills to do this either partially or completely.
3. The small minority of situations where people seek, or their behaviour creates, outcomes that are contrary to legislation and regulation, or are a serious risk to their well-being or that of others, and where compulsory intervention may become necessary.

Conflicts at all levels (the service user, the professionals, the public and the media) about the outcomes are most likely to be contested in this latter group. However, they are likely to exist in all interventions and conflicts of opinion and judgement should be recorded and monitored in the intervention plans.

Areas of Social Work Intervention

A long-standing conundrum is 'what level of need should have attention from the state?' Statements on values refer to the rights of individuals, and there is a move to try and establish a 'right to independent living'. In practice, provision and intervention are limited by:

- resources (expertise, provision, time, money)

- priorities of the organisation, those of others contributing to integrated services, national and local policies
- different conceptions of the role of social welfare
- the role social work plays outside the boundaries of social welfare.

The need for social work intervention through state supported organisations is always politically shaped, but there are a growing number of employment opportunities for social workers that are extending the funding sources beyond the welfare budget. For example, as independent social workers, in education, health, employment services, industry, government and the media. When asking questions about the need for social work intervention, it is essential first to know what political decisions have been made about the function of social welfare systems in meeting need. Hardiker et al. discuss five levels of intervention she identified in 1997 and the nature of need they address in children, young people and their families. The model could be adapted to apply to adults. The levels are:

- *Base level:* needs in the general population for whom universal services are provided.
- *First levels:* vulnerable groups which may be enabled to use universal services and are targeted through initiatives such as Sure Start.
- *Second levels:* early stresses and families in temporary crisis assisted by short-term interventions and resources. Hardiker locates 'children in need here.
- *Third levels:* serious stresses including risks of serious harm and family breakdown which need intervention to restore family functioning.
- *Fourth levels:* covers a diverse group of issues: social breakdown, children looked after, children abused

within the care system; methods include therapy, damage limitation and permanency planning'.

Using a grid she demonstrates how different models of welfare and the levels of intervention interact. If the state takes a minimal approach, its services will not come into play until the third level is reached. If the state is committed to combating social disadvantage, interventions will be apparent at the first level. In this framework it is our view that social work is most usually needed, to varying degrees, from the second to the fourth levels.

Decisions about the Need for Social Work Intervention

The social policy objective of social work intervention is that it should be tailored to a specific situation and that each person is unique. Social work is a collective activity and is consequently dependent on partnerships; not least because many of the resources required are outwith social work. While some partnerships are very successful, they are in general notoriously difficult to set up and maintain without one partner becoming dominant. There is also no evidence that colocating different professionals will in itself lead to improved outcomes for people using services, although it can improve the effectiveness of systems.

Partnerships between different organisations and local people are difficult enough, but they also require agreements about the function of social work within neighbourhood renewal and community capacity building. In the main this does not exist in spite of the inclusion of community development in the responsibilities of Social Work Departments. This is unsatisfactory because community development is effective in facilitating the building of the community's capacity to address both collective and individual problems.

Decisions about Social Work Intervention

Social work intervention should take place only when the situation is not 'straight forward'. Routine social care responses should be through self assessment or by using social care, education, housing or health care workers with a lower level of training and skill.

The requirement for social work intervention is triggered by a number of factors such as:

Differences of opinion about what constitutes a social problem

This changes over time. For example,

- until relatively recently domestic violence was accepted within marriage and other personal relationships between men and women. Evidence that domestic violence indicates a risk of violence towards children and witnessing abuse is emotionally and psychologically damaging to children and young people has moved domestic violence from a private event, to a child protection concern
- drug and alcohol abuse is now a significant social problem. It impacts on the next generation of children through a failure to parent adequately and the likelihood of birth impairments
- child prostitution is now defined as child abuse rather than the consequence of the immoral behaviour of a young person.
- racial abuse and homophobic behaviour was endemic in our communities and institutions, but policies state that intervention is necessary.

At points of change social work intervention is necessary to innovate or spread examples of good practice that have existed in isolated pockets.

Service user groups where there are contentious issues

For a number of groups the imperative to promote people's rights has to be balanced with other considerations. For example:

- when a criminal offence is likely to be, or has been, committed
- when behaviour is disruptive of the life of a community, harasses or is dangerous for others
- when the child or adult needs to be kept safe from harm.

Although this represents a minority of people who need social work interventions, they are high profile. Social workers and their managers are often required to justify their action or inaction to the public, politicians and the media. Intervention is usually multi-organisational and multi-professional. A battlefield often exists between support, rehabilitation, retribution and punishment. Professional judgements about risks and the possibility of change and public views may be in conflict with each other, even though prison is not a good predictor of changed behaviour on discharge.

To operate effectively in these areas at social workers need skills:

- in working with the bounds of confidentiality at the same time as explaining to the media and the public what they are doing in ways that are neither mysterious nor patronising,
- demonstrating that they are accountable for what they are doing in accessible language as part of social care governance.

Who is the client

Most referrals to social work services are made by other professionals, organisations, relatives, neighbours and friends, and not the individual who is the subject of concern. Social workers, and the organisations within which they work are subject to multiple systems of accountability. A clear understanding of who see themselves, and who are seen, as the potential beneficiaries of a particular social work intervention is essential. Without this the intervention can be seen to have failed, even if the service users themselves are satisfied.

Thresholds of need These vary between service user groups and according to:

- the availability of resources (money, staff time and expertise),
- guidance and procedures about the assessment of need and risk
- judgements exercised by social workers and their managers and other professionals based on organisational priorities
- the support available to the service user within their own social network or their community
- different thresholds existing in voluntary or private organisation or between statutory organisations
- political priorities and the funding that flows from these.

The variability of thresholds means that there are significant gaps in coverage for groups of people with similar needs that cannot be explained by the support available through their family or social network. Although disabled children are defined as children in need, a substantial number are not known to social services. People with similar levels of Alzheimer's Disease to those in residential provision are living in the community. Their family carers may or may not receive services.

People with sensory impairments can become housebound, and consequently more susceptible to depression, because they cannot cope with the environment or be sure that buses stop near enough the pavement for them to feel confident in using them, they are vulnerable to falls and accidents. This knowledge could contribute to health, social and environmental policies on prevention and reducing social exclusion.

Risks to the safety of the individual, their family or the public

The nation and local state has a clear responsibility to protect children and young people. A similar responsibility holds in relation to those committing offences. In both these cases there are clear procedures that involve a combination of professional assessments with the ultimate decisions made by the courts. Where adults present a risk to themselves this is more problematic. There are human rights issues when the individual is legally competent to make decisions about their lives. These groups include those who threaten to take their own lives, have a mental illness or learning disabilities and do not want social work or health interventions in their lives. Some may refuse treatment, or, have been treated but fail to take medication. They may be concerned about side effects or have a chaotic life style.

There are many individuals abusing illegal drugs who are not prosecuted. Often no social work intervention occurs either because there are insufficient resources or expertise and/or because there is recognition the behaviour is chronic and not likely to change. Insufficient attention is given to the fact that many people using social work services have multiple impairments that interact with each other. The drug abusers may have been abused as children, be parents, be homeless, have a mental health difficulty or face all of these difficulties at the same or at different points in their lives. Although there are multi professional forums and procedures it is often social workers or the criminal justice system that copes with chronic difficulties arising from abuse.

Concerns about the capacity of individuals to have control over their lives or to keep themselves or their child/ren safe

Judgements about whether individuals can keep themselves safe from harm and live independently are often very fine. Rightly there is an emphasis on their human rights and respect for people's wishes. Examples include:

- people with chronic mental health conditions, people abusing drugs and alcohol, people with Alzheimer's Disease.
- sensory impairment which increase with age and is often combined with depression or other mental health problems
- people with learning disabilities can find that their capacity to live independently is reducing as their life expectancy increases. The level of social care – as opposed to housing - support they need because of physical impairments increases at an earlier age than for the general population. We are in relatively uncharted waters in planning services that are appropriate for this group of people. Social work intervention, combined with health and housing assessments, is required to monitor the effectiveness of the personalised package of support in keeping the person safe from harm and to respond to often quite subtle changes that indicate a higher level of support is necessary.

The evidence about outcomes

Evidence about which social work interventions work in what situations is always likely to be tentative because there are so many variables. As in parts of medicine there are numerous circumstances in which random controlled trials are not possible. Many health predictions are for whole patient populations, rather than certainty about the effect of a specific treatment on a particular patient. Success is defined within time limits rather than for cure of an illness or condition. A growing amount of information is available about outcomes of social work and social care interventions that can assist workers and managers in reaching decisions about what responses are most likely to succeed. These include such soft data as the personality of the worker and their attention to the process.

Perspective on the Need for Social Work Intervention

The way social work interventions are implemented is not neutral or value free. There have been huge changes within social work of attitudes towards people using services. A leading social worker in the United States 1930s depression commented:

> We as social workers saw for the first time was that people like ourselves in backgrounds social status, education and mores... were suddenly subject to circumstances that despite our lip service to the contrary we had reserved for people who were not like us.

Subsequently women, people from black and minority ethnic groups, gays and lesbians complained social work was deeply paternalistic, racist and homophobic. By the 1980s disabled people challenged the way the application of social work theory dis-empowered them and argued for citizen participation. These positions were then regarded as anything from dangerous to misguided by many.

Conflicts and uncertainty are endemic in social work and can arise from:

- the level of complexity involved
- different views about what has happened, what is needed to achieve a good outcome
- who is, or thinks they should be, the beneficiary of any intervention
- conflicts of interest
- uncertainty about the risks involved and the outcomes that can be achieved
- moral and ethical dilemmas

Service User and Carers

This section uses evidence from either research undertaken by people using services, or based on the views of people using services. In the context of user involvement in matching needs and services for children and young people, Tunnard reported:

> [Users] have clear views about the social work task they want to see preserved and promoted: early attention to problems to avoid more intrusive action later on; continued advocacy from social workers over health, housing, social security and education problems; and respite measures so that parents and children can get a break from one another or children can get temporary relief from neglectful parents or impoverished surroundings.

In social work with children and families, the most contentious area is where control functions are used because the abilities of a parent/s to care for their children are deemed to have fallen below acceptable levels, or where interventions arise from concerns about an individual's safety or the risk they pose to others. This has become the best-known form of social work intervention, and colours the public's view of seeking or accepting involvement with social workers.

Amongst the adult groups, the clearest account of how service users define needs comes from the disability movement and its development of the social model.

Key to this perspective is the understanding that needs for support and assistance come not so much from people's impairments, but mainly as a result of the obstacles society and the environment place in the way of their leading the lives they choose. These barriers limit or prevent them from taking charge of their lives, exercising choice and participating fully in the educational, employment, family and social activities non-disabled people take for granted.

Advocates of the social model argue that social work assessment should shift from focusing on what people cannot do, their degree of dependency and their eligibility for services, to addressing how the barriers to independence can be removed and what support will give people better access to mainstream activities and ability to manage their own lives. Social work intervention may include enabling people to access information, direct payments and other funding, communication, assistive technology, personal assistance, and mainstream educational, employment, housing and health services. It may also involve support to challenge discrimination and stigma, to enforce legal and civil rights such as those relating to disabled people's access to jobs, goods and services, and to promote their rights to privacy, family life and participation in civic society.

Initially established in the disability field, approaches reflecting the social model have been applied in mental health and in learning disabilities. Except for family carers who are partners, women form the largest majority of family carers. The failure to provide them with sufficient support adds a potential strain on the social work services since their contribution is estimated in the UK to be the equivalent of £000000, and the highest points of risk of admission to residential care for older people is when the primary family carer is sick or dies.

It is often carers, whether family, friends and neighbours, or staff in social work services and primary health care, who initiate social work intervention in relation to people with learning disabilities, older people and young people with disabilities or mental health problems. For individuals and their carers the main considerations will tend to be need for:

- information, advice and support at times of transition – when young people move from children's to adults' services, when older people are no longer able to cope at home without assistance, when parents of learning disabled adults look ahead to the time when they will no longer be able to provide care and support
- assistance in finding their way round complex multi-agency structures of assessment, prioritising, resource allocation, service provision and purchase, in order to put together flexible packages of support or get access to scarce or specialist services
- assistance where there may be conflicts of interest between service users and their carers – whether different opinions about the best way forward, competing needs in areas like respite and risk, family and relationship stress and tension, or potential or actual abuse of one or more vulnerable people.

Front line Social Workers

Front line social workers often complain that they do not use the skills for which they were trained. The emphasis on assessment to determine eligibility and dealing with high risk diverts attention from preventative and therapeutic work. The front line is the point of interaction between social workers and people using services and whatever the policy statements say, this is where the words either become a reality in the lives of people using services or remain words on paper. Using an outcomes approach, social workers can define whether they and the service users are working towards:

— maintaining the current level of a person's, group's or community's quality of life and social and emotional well-being, or to try to slow down deterioration in it. This maintenance work will be a continuing task - throughout assessment, care planning, therapeutic interventions, monitoring and review to enable adjustment to changing needs
— to achieve a change in the quality of their lives
— to evaluate the impact of the process of the service, that is how it is delivered rather than what is provided.

National Policy on Well-being and Regeneration

The context within which social work operates and the agenda for the foreseeable future is broadly set within a public health or well-being agenda. This strategic approach focuses on improving the economy and social life through investment in individuals, families groups and communities. Based on evidence from a range of disciplines, effective intervention involves an integrated multi organisational and multi-professional response.

A key focus is reducing or removing blocks to life-long education and training, health, community development and neighbourhood renewal. The principles, methods of promoting involvement and participation and social inclusion overlap with those of social work. Both share an emphasis on facilitating empowerment, people taking control over their own lives, building commitment to and ownership of the process of change. Social work could add skills to these interventions particularly for socially excluded groups who are often seen as a part of the problem rather than part of the solution. The evidence is that local people experience being marginalised or excluded entirely from decision making.

Work such as Charles Leadbeater's *Personalisation through participation: a new script for public services* has modernised the language of the public health agenda. Leadbeater points out that in the past improvement was often achieved through the state providing services – clean water, health and safety, sewage - but that in the 21st century governments also have a responsibility to provide 'platforms' or 'environments' that enable citizens to take as much control as possible over the management of problem solving in their lives. Drawing heavily on social care research and development, he argues:

> The key is to build up the knowledge and the confidence of the users to take action themselves, to self manage their health without turning to professionals.

Social work has the skills to promote the participation of socially excluded groups, to manage change, negotiate conflicts and build on capacity. However, this has to be seen as a significant function and not one than is residual to be undertaken in the spaces between rationing scarce resources through assessment and managing risk. A shift is required in the conception social work among politicians and the public. The framework of social work education in Scotland provides a sound base for developing the workforce in this direction as opposed to it being the individual choice of career option for some social workers.

The National Framework, the National Occupational Standards that underpin the qualification for Social Work in England, Northern Ireland and Wales, and the Codes of Practice for Social Care Staff provide the boundaries for the values, knowledge and skills for social workers in Scotland. Legislation on the responsibilities of Social Work Departments and the roles of social workers in the delivery of these responsibilities identify which needs must be responded to. Broadly, these concern the safety of the individual and that of others. These are the control functions of social work: that is where social work interventions are required because:

- minimum expectations of parenting capacity have not been met
- the individual belongs to a group defined as vulnerable and needing protection
- the behaviour of the individual is creating a risk to themselves or to others or seems to pose a threat to the life of the community.

Whilst this remit is national, thresholds differ and acceptable risks will depend both on formal and informal support systems in local communities. For example, in a rural area, a person with learning disabilities or mental health problems may be seen to present less of a threat, or none at all, because they are known as an individual. The same behaviour may be seen very differently in an inner city area where the person is not known. Social work has to be able to recognise, and act according to, the distinctions between these different contexts.

For over forty years it has been recognised that social work intervention cannot be seen in isolation and that it is dependent on the infrastructure provided through income and employment, health, housing, education, transport and the local environment. These resources are also the priorities for people using services.

It is essential that social work does not over promise and under deliver. Social work suffers from a history of either not stating what an intervention is intended to achieve or of presenting itself as 'the solution' to a social problem. A more cautious approach exists in health where definitions of success are circumscribed by the evidence about its effectiveness for general populations rather than outcomes for individual patients. Estimations of success in social work must be measured against the level of damage that a person has to overcome whether this is the result of emotional or sexual abuse, serious relationship problems, poor parenting.

In many cases statutory agencies are not in a position to say 'no' when change is impossible. There should be greater emphasis in future of identifying where the outcome is likely to be at best stabilisation or the alleviation of the effects on the individual and the family. This is similar to health where it is impossible to treat serious conditions and efforts are made to alleviate pain and distress or to slow down deterioration.

Evidence based practice should provide a sounder basis for identifying achievable outcomes from social work interventions and therefore assist in focusing expectations and input. It is equally important to hold on to the capacity for hope because confidence, self-esteem and positive attitudes in both people using services and workers can achieve outcomes against evidence of what it was reasonable to expect. The capacity to convey hope and belief in a person are components that resist measurement.

A frequently omitted element in satisfaction of people using services is the personality of the social worker or care worker involved – something that is difficult to educate or train a person in, though existing characteristics can be enhanced. The implementation of policies to the extent that their impact is noticed by people using services and by social workers requires the management of change in organisations and people. The management of change is usefully divided into:

- *First order change*: this is incremental change within the rule of the existing system
- *Second order change*: is when there is a change in the rules that requires a change in the nature of the system itself.

Current policies require second order change, with impacts on multiple systems and on the skills and expertise valued. What at an earlier point was a highly valued skill can become a block to implementation. Over the past 30 years Social Work Departments have undergone substantial change as have the expectations and training of the workers within them. There remain remnants of the past in systems and in the minds of workers from each generation. Some will welcome innovation because it allows them to do the work they always wanted to do. Others will resist because their power or professional identity is threatened, or because they lack the confidence or the capacity to meet the new demands.

There is a multiplicity of organisational and professional stages and positions that have to be worked with, rather than a monolithic unity that has to be managed. Part of this is a persistent strand of resources and approaches that are service rather than needs led. Some time lags relate to the lengthy process of shifting resources, including buildings and staffing, into new areas. Others concern the time taken to embed innovations: years rather than months. Direct Payments is a very good example of second order change. Implementation has been slower than hoped. Growth has been in the 'safer' areas such work with disabled people who led the demand for and developed the expertise in using Direct Payments. It has been less successful in reaching people with learning disabilities, sensory impairments or older people. In part, the explanation is lack of information among first line and middle management who act as gate keepers to innovations and also to a failure to connect Direct Payments with a new conception of the rights of people using services.

International Definition of Social Work

A third framework is the international definition of social work agreed between the Schools of Social Work and the International Federation of Social Workers:

> Social work is a profession which promotes social change, problem solving in human relationships and the empowerment and liberation of people to enhance well-being. Utilising theories of human behaviour and social systems, social work intervenes at points where people interact with their environments. Principles of human rights and social justice are fundamental to social work.

This takes a very broad perspective on the role of social work. Conceptions of social work's role in promoting human rights and social justice

- differ between countries and at different times in the same country,
- whether it is a legitimate activity when people have been trained often with financial support from, and subsequently employed by, state institutions.

All the above perspectives view social work intervention as more than an administrative task. Quality and effectiveness are achieved through how that service or support is provided: the process and the relationship are integral to the service and sometimes a service in itself.

> They must also be responsive to the people who use them and must treat them with respect. The more people feel valued within their community, the more likely it is that they community itself will develop the capacity to thrive.
>
> Personalisation is just as simple (as privatisation) by putting users at the heart of services, enabling them to become participants in the design and delivery, services will be more effective by mobilising millions of people as co-producers of the public goods they value.

Conflicts between Perspectives on the Need for Social Work Intervention

Much social work intervention is concerned with managing conflicts between the different perspectives on the need for social work intervention. When social work was seen as promoting a dependency culture the consequence was that the role was deliberately circumscribed. This view was in conflict with the perception that social workers had of themselves and their purpose. Throughout the UK there has been a growing consistency between the perspectives of people using services and policy positions. It is much harder to hold to this consistency in practice. Often conflicts between policies, resources and requirements are resolved only at the front line. Some of these conflicts could and should be resolved by management and others are contradictions that have to be lived with at all levels. An outcomes approach to social work intervention and an emphasis on personalisation and person centred planning requires greater openness about conflicts and the way they are resolved.

Conflicts arising from interventions relating to control functions

Although a separate project is addressing offending behaviour, the control functions of social work cannot be ignored in this project, because it is a significant source of conflicts of perspective between social workers and:

- parents who are abusing drugs or alcohol in relation to decisions to remove their children,
- mental health survivors over compulsory admissions,
- people with learning disabilities where individuals have committed offences,
- members of the community who disagree with assessments that the risks to the safety of the

individual and/ to others are within acceptable limits.

When the exercise of social work control functions fail this is often seen to be the result of misjudgements or interventions that were too limited, involvement too late or non-existent. The failure of social work interventions may result from a lack of skills and knowledge, or from organisational priorities including allocating sufficient time for the work, or be the result of an insufficient supply of, or inappropriate resources or expertise, a lack of evidence on which to act. It may equally be a mixture of all of these. Social work is not alone in coping with the consequences of the failure to control. This situation affects other professions, such as doctors and sheriffs and the police and there are systems in place to address these failures. However, social work probably suffers more than these professions from a tendency for condemnation to spread from the specific failure to the profession as a whole. The establishment of regulatory organisations for social work and social care may in time give the public confidence in the profession.

Conflicts arising from implicit or explicit disagreements about problems and outcomes

The history of social work is littered with evidence that there can be a huge gap between the judgements of social workers and those of people using services. This is a problem that has not been resolved. A consistent finding of research led by people using services is that social workers do not listen to them even though this skill is given high priority in social work education. Nichols et al argue that identifying different perspectives on an issue or problem and having clarity about the service user's 'preferred option' is essential to addressing the noise that enters the interaction between the worker and the people using services. Some of this comes from very well intentioned standards, procedures, policies of the organisation and the profession that divert the worker away from listening to the explanations, experience and expertise of the people concerned.

Conflicts arising from complexity and contradictions

Social workers intervene where the issues are complex and where these contradictions are likely to be in evident.

> Social workers work in complex social situations to protect individuals and groups and promote their well-being.....social work is a moral activity in the sense that social workers make and follow difficult decisions about human situations that directly benefit or harm an individual or group. They should be able to understand moral reasoning and to make decisions in difficult ethical situations, especially where there are conflicting moral obligations.

In much of their work social workers have to find reasoned and responsible solutions amid a maze of values:

- the profession's own values
- society's predominant values as set down in legislation
- society's conflicting values - expressed by vocal minorities and held by powerless majorities
- other professions' values - health, medicine, education
- the local community's values
- the extended family's values
- the nuclear family's values
- the individual's values.

A high level of skill is required to identify conflicts, their origins and to negotiate outcomes that are frequently a compromise between what is preferred and what is possible within available resources, the balance of the rights and expectations of the individual and those of others involved and to negotiate an agreement (including disagreements) about a viable course of action. The level of the expertise required can be missed because the immediate location is often mundane – a person's home, in a car, during an activity such as cooking, filling in a form. Similarly, it is this very ordinariness of the situation that can obscure conflicts in perspective.

Working within and between Organisations

Social work intervention alone is rarely sufficient. It is dependent on trying to create the conditions within which change or maintenance outcomes can be achieved. Usually this requires securing agreements and resources from within and outside the social worker's organisation and profession. For example:

Within the organisation negotiation is necessary:

- to make and implement a plan for permanence for an accommodated child
- to get support from the mental health team for a parent to continue to care for her child
- to fund support for a carer of a person with learning disabilities or Alzheimer's Disease
- for a disabled person to achieve greater independence through Direct Payments.

Outwith the organisation negotiation is necessary with:

- the police to protect a black or minority ethnic family from racial harassment
- health services to secure health care for an elderly person whose condition has deteriorated
- private and voluntary care homes to provide a home for an older person

- a housing support organisation to arrange independent living for a person with learning disabilities, or to negotiate changes in the level of support because the individuals social care needs or health needs have increased.

Negotiating for resources within or outwith the organisation, or supporting others to do this, is carried out routinely by all levels of social worker. This is often described 'working the system'. It could, and we argue should, be seen as an intervention necessary to ensure that the organisation delivers its primary objectives as often as possible. One member of our team worked in an authority where the computer system failed two or three times a week. It was not until it was framed in terms of a potential child death that the computer team understood their contribution to the safety of children.

An understanding of group dynamics in team working is necessary in multi-skilled/ professional teams as a means of enabling them to function effectively. The more social work intervention becomes a collective, rather than an individual, activity the more these group work skills will be required:

- for building, maintaining, disbanding work based teams. These often include not only agency workers but also members whose life experience, professional training and work experience have been in a variety of countries. For this group their time in Scotland is intended to be time limited before they resume their career in their own country.
- for teams to be inclusive of service users and carers.
- to create ad hoc teams to deliver personalised services, whose membership is routinely changing so that they are fit for purpose. They are as likely to include parents and family carers as other professional groups.

- to keep the focus on the work as opposed to being diverted into conflicts between team members or relative professional status.
- to build and maintain community partnerships that are experienced as inclusive by people using services and their organisations rather than empty words.

These tasks are not exclusive to social work, but require seeing effective team and inter organisational working as part of the professional task.

Understanding human relationships, individual learning patterns, group dynamics and the way power operates, contributes to improving poor team performance, but also to the maintenance and development of effective teams. Scotland's expansion of social care involves a growing demand for social care skills and retaining existing and attracting new staff is a key task for organisations.

User Led Organisations, Voluntary Organisatons, Community Groups and Private Companies

Organisations providing social care are diverse not only in their specific focus, but also in their governance, structures and priorities. How consistent the day to day practice is with the aspiration for user centred outcomes or personalisation will depend on the remit and purposes of the organisation. Coherence between an organisation's remit and its front line practice requires a culture that supports practice and learning, including learning from mistakes, and taking risks. The maintenance of this culture requires constant attention and in common with good practice is easily lost.

In service user organisations there is likely to be a high level of consistency between the perspectives of services users and the purposes of the organisation.

Where a voluntary organisation is self funded this level of consistency may also be retained within the limits of available funds and the stated charitable purposes. This position of secure independence is relatively rare, since most voluntary organisations will be commissioned by a local authority to provide services according to contract with evidence provided that this has been achieved. A similar situation applies in private companies.

There is consistent evidence that mainstream services frequently fail to provide support that is culturally appropriate for people from black and minority ethnic groups. For black run organisations interventions are necessary to create the space for culturally competent practice. Interventions on the part of the manager to work with the majority population, with funders and statutory organisations were routinely required to enable front line workers to offer culturally appropriate interventions.

Need for Change in Social Work Interventions

There are four main reasons for the need to change.

1. *Policy changes resulting in a change in status of people using services to citizens:* Interventions have been based on assumptions that people using services were recipients. They focused on what individuals could not do as opposed to what they and their social network could do. A model based on full and equal citizenship requires interventions in which people using services are active and equal participants.
2. *Changes in the knowledge and skill base:* As with any profession there are both new approaches and new understandings about the effectiveness of specific interventions. Investment in research and the dissemination of knowledge and skills in health

remains vast greater than in social care. But the strengthening of these resources in social work and social care should result in more knowledge based practice and management in the medium term. The case for recognising different sources of knowledge has been made and the multiplicity of information collected in Departments needs to include that produced through the experience and expertise of people using services and front line workers as well as from research.

3. *Technological and structural changes:* Given rapid changes, gaps in knowledge and skills may arise because new areas of work are emerging resulting in supply falling behind the demands. Examples of this in the past have included the emergence of HIV/AIDs, working with asylum seekers, the role of social work in disasters. New technologies and the growing familiarity of the public in using them opens up new forms of interventions particularly to assist independent living and at the lower levels of need. In areas where there is rapid development or new issues practice is of necessity in advance of theory. Strategies in these circumstances include:
   - transferring existing knowledge and skills to the new area
   - drawing on any international experience and expertise
   - networking to share and learn from experience.
   - research on needs and effective responses.

   Initially these may need to be done separately to structure different a perspective before it is possible to bring experience and learning together in new ways.

4. Multi organisational, multi disciplinary teams and multi professional teams will be the norm A

consequence is that greater attention will have to be given to:

- supporting professional social work practice
- safeguarding the value base, the relationship and the process as essential to good practice
- charting new and emerging groupings of skills and expertise of social workers and related occupations and professions. Some will merit attention at post qualifying levels, some will be idiosyncratic and fit for purpose only in a very limited number of circumstances.

3

Social Work Practices in a Globalised World

Social work has always been international. Recently it has become more so; a trend that continues. Social work education is an important focus in international social work.

Social work is a product of modernism in Western states as industrialised economies developed in the late 19th century. That is, it emerged from an idealist belief that the state could overcome social problems, using science and knowledge to resolve social problems. In most countries, therefore, it is part of state services and claims a rational evidence as the basis of its practice. In rich Western countries social work is substantially part of the state: it is organised public welfare provision. This is so even where services are offered by profit or not-for-profit organisations, because they are mainly funded by states. Its commitment to science means that social work as a profession and as a way of intervening in people's lives relies on the assumption that it can develop universal knowledge. Such knowledge seeks to provide explanation and understanding about human beings, their behaviour and their society.

The idea is that universal knowledge will apply to everyone, in whatever culture or society they live.

Therefore, it can provide firm evidence for deciding how best to act when intervening with any human beings. Relying on a claim to universal knowledge assumes, uncritically, that such knowledge may be transferred from Western societies in which most of it is developed to societies in the South with markedly different cultures and access to resources.

In the 21st century, globalisation leads to changes that challenge social work practice and education, and the idea of postmodernism challenges the validity of a universal knowledge base. This is because where societies are built on different cultural and social assumptions postmodernism raises questions about the dominance of any particular set of ideas, both generally and in social work. Postmodernism proposes that social phenomena such as social work vary according to the social and historical context in which they operate. An international social work, therefore, raises questions about whether Western models of social work practice and organisation are universal in their application.

Among the most important consequences of the development of postmodern, globalised social works is inequality within and across societies. This is important because inequalities create social strains between different groups and psychological stresses for individuals.

Social work has a commitment to social justice. Social work that deals only with psychological problems fails to handle the consequences of unfairness and inequality and with social factors that lead to the problems. Social processes that create inequality and injustice constantly change. This means that practice and education need to be aware of inequalities created by new social trends, to understand them and how they affect individuals and communities.

INTERNATIONAL SOCIAL WORK

Most social work students, educators and practitioners do not cross national borders in their work. International social work refers to a number of different activities:

- *Working in development agencies in the South* – Examples of development agencies might be non-governmental organisations (NGOs) like Save the Children, Caritas, and Médicin Sans Frontiéres. Many people make careers in international agencies working in the South, or commit parts of their lives when they are young, as 'time out' or in retirement to such work. In some countries, development work in the South would not be considered social work, while elsewhere it would.
- *Working for official international agencies* – Examples of international agencies might include a range of United Nations agencies, the European Commission or aid departments of national governments. As with development agencies, there would be similar differences in how such work is viewed; in the United Kingdom of Great Britain and Northern Ireland (UK) and some other countries, work in such agencies would not be viewed as social work. Working for agencies dealing with cross-national issues – Examples might be agencies dealing with international adoption or family matters such as abduction of a child from one legal jurisdiction in family disputes. Some service user organisations, for example for disabled and mentally ill people, have staff working on international links.
- *Working for international social work organisations* – Examples might be the International Federation of Social Workers (IFSW) and the International Association of School of Social Work (IASSW) or

people employed in countries on projects for or linking with such organisations.

- Participating in international conferences, educational or professional visits, exchanges and placements and research;
- Working as a social worker in a country that is foreign to them;
- Working with refugees and immigrants in their own country.

In the South, social workers will often experience directly poverty, inequalities and social and personal problems that arise from the impact of globalisation in their societies. Even though the average Western practitioner does not work internationally, daily practice may lead them to experience some of the local consequences of globalisation: international migration, asylum seeking, and refugees. They may also experience concern about forced marriage, cultural conflicts and terrorism that are a product of the social trends of globalisation. The uncertainty about how to evaluate and respond to them emerges from the impact of postmodern ideas in Western societies.

In Western countries, where social work originated and developed most strongly, and where it is most firmly established. However, it is developing fast in a diverse range of other countries – in Africa, China, Eastern European countries – that have little connection with and reliance on Western culture and social structures. Inevitably, those developments in other countries and cultures challenge dominant Western ways of thinking about social work.

This interaction in these ways:

- Western social work is not necessarily relevant to non-Western countries and its relevance should always be challenged.

- Western social work should be influenced by non-Western social work, which will inevitably have different values and practices. Nevertheless, Western cultural and economic power means that we have to establish ways for it to achieve that influence.
- Non-Western countries should and do create their own social works, and may, but should not need to, compare them with or justify them against Western values and practices.

A worldwide view of social work might be richer if it included ideas from and perceptions in non-Western countries. For example, Graham's work on African worldviews suggests alternative perspectives on family and community that might lead Western social workers to value shared experience and collective spiritual, family and community engagement in resolving social and personal problems. Western cultural, economic and social power has given social work ideas from the West too much influence in other countries and cultures.

The fact that there are international social work organisations suggests that there is an international social work. This has been promoted over the years by an 'internationalist view' held by activists in the international social work organisations, particularly IFSW and IASSW. It may be seen, for example, in the successive reports about social work education across the world by Alice Salomon, Eileen Younghusband, and Katherine Kendall. The international view proposes that there is one diverse social work, with local variations, rather than local social works that share some common elements.

Around the millennium, the international associations began to pursue these projects by devising and promoting an international definition of social work, and international standards for education and training in social work. Sewpaul, a significant figure in the education project, accepts that postmodernism challenges such endeavours towards a 'grand narrative' of social work. Gray suggests that there is a risk that promoting global standards for social work education may lead to Western models of practice being seen as universal ideals to be reached. She notes that it may be possible to consider an international model of practice or education as a touchstone for comparisons, without trying to gain international agreement to definition or standards.

There are different forms of social work with different cultural roots, rather than variations on a common social work. Walton and el Nasr suggested that two parallel processes of interaction between international and local forms of social work may occur:

- indigenisation of non-local social work practice, by adapting imported ideas to make them relevant to local practice;
- authentisation of local practices to form a new locally-relevant structure of ideas.

Gray argues that indigenisation is a cross-cultural practice. However, it may be an outgrowth of the history of colonialism, since it works from a largely Western conception of practice.

Gray and Fook propose that in considering international social work, four tensions, between:

- globalisation and localisation – the tendency for globalising and localising tendencies to occur together
- Westernisation and indigenisation – the balance between Western and alternative conceptions of practice
- multiculturalism and universalisation – the implication and response to inbuilt cultural biases

– universal-local standards – the incorporation of both universal and localised conceptualisations of social work within our thinking.

It is important to examine the issues represented in these tensions. Some argue that they are not necessarily oppositions. Sewpaul for example, sees a universal definition of social work and a universal standard for social work education as assisting the integration of social work into countries where it is underdeveloped or insecure. In this way, universal and local standards can support each other. Similarly, Western approaches may become a touchstone against which local practices may be authentised.

Nimmagadda and Cowger's study of authentisation and indigenisation in Indian social work agencies is an example of such a process. They look at how Western practices such as giving advice, family intervention, confrontation and reassurance are adapted by Indian social expectations and concepts of Dharma and Karma. For example, mainly female workers, who were not expected to act assertively, were not always able to confront the behaviour of mainly male alcoholics, as Western social workers would. Advice-giving, which was contrary to Western social work values of self-determination and non-directiveness, was accepted because Indian values acknowledge the duty of workers to take authority in particular situations.

In short, the social workers need an understanding of international social work as part of their profession. Even if they are not international social workers themselves, their daily practice and the needs and problems that users of their services face will be affected by international social trends. Students and educators will also be aware that the international element in the literature and practice that they study questions universal validity of knowledge and practice.

4

Social Work Strategies against Racism

Social work as a profession aims to address the impact of social problems on the lives of individuals, families, groups, organisations, and communities. To achieve this, the members of the profession, the organisations through which they work, and the schools of social work must have the knowledge base, theories, and values to understand relevant social issues, especially for the purpose of creating positive change.

Institutional/Structural Racism

Institutional or structural racism, defined as the social, economic, educational, and political forces or policies that operate to foster discriminatory outcomes or give preferences to members of one group over others, derives its genesis from the origins of race as a concept. Race as a biological fact has been invalidated by biologists and geneticists, but race as a social construct is very real. Physical traits still have meaning as markers of social race identity. It is this social race identity that confers placement in the social hierarchy of society, and thereby access to or denial of privileges, power, and wealth. "The status assignment based on skin color identity has evolved into complex social structures that promote a power differential between Whites and various people-of-color". The emphasis on the use of physical features to classify and group people has its history from

> the extended encounter between European and non-European peoples that began in the late 15th and early 16th centuries. Discovering human beings in Asia, Africa, and the Americas who looked- and often acted- very different from themselves, Europeans concluded that these superficial differences were surely indicators of much more fundamental differences as well. This conclusion helped them to colonise, enslave, and even exterminate certain of those peoples. Europeans came to believe that races are in fact distinct and identifiable human groups; that there are systematic, inherited, biological differences among races; and that the non-White races are innately inferior to Whites-that is, to Europeans.

In the United States, the cognitive dissonance between the values and beliefs of the Protestant founders for human rights, liberty, justice, democracy, brotherhood, and equality alongside the practice of enslavement of Africans, the making of Mexican/Mexican Americans a foreign minority in the land of their birth, and genocide of Native Americans was resolved by classifying groups of people by virtue of their physical characteristics as being not only different, but innately inferior and thereby unworthy of rights and entitlements. From the very origins of this nation, the concept of race was used to institutionalise the benefits of one group of people while denying them to other groups of people.

The determination of who is or is not white in America has fluctuated over time. There have been times and places in which the Irish, Jews, Italians, and Latinos have been considered white or non-white. The changes in the U.S. Census Bureau nomenclature system over time demonstrate the fluidness in the U.S. society's perceptions of how people should be clustered. The categorisation that had been "White/Non-White" is now a set of five major groups along with notation of national origin. Furthermore, the individual determines his or her own race and can choose more than one. The census also makes a clear demarcation between racial categories and the ethnic category of Latino/Hispanic who can be of any race.

Contemporary United States continues to struggle with the cognitive dissonance between the espoused virtuous beliefs of this nation and its actual practices in relationship to those who are "different," meaning "not white." These struggles are captured in several of the terms often associated with a discussion of racism and related concepts.

Overt Racism

Racism is the practice of discrimination and prejudice based on racial classification supported by the power to enforce that prejudice. Ethnocentrism is the view that one's own group is the center of everything and that all things are judged based on one's own group. Prejudice is the negative (or positive/idealised) attitudes, thoughts, and beliefs about an entire category of people formed without full knowledge or examination of the facts. And discrimination is acting on the basis of prejudice.

Discrimination is often codified by laws, regulations, and rules. People experience oppression when they are deprived of human rights or dignity and are (or feel) powerless to do anything about it. Sometimes the negative act is in the form of exclusion, in which people are denied the opportunity to participate in a certain right, benefit, or privilege. Sometimes the negative act is in the form of marginalisation, in which people find that they are on the fringe of political, social, or economic consciousness. That sense of invisibility results in decisions being made by those in power that may be harmful simply because the needs were not considered. Assimilation means being absorbed into the cultural tradition of the dominant society and consequently losing one's historical identity.This is in contrast to acculturation in which there is an adaptation to a different culture but retention of original identity.

Social Work Response

These concepts are relatively familiar to most social workers, and many view their work as addressing various aspects of these problems. As a profession, social work "has traditionally been looked to for leadership and support in altering conditions that impede human potential and dignity". Social work organisations can easily point to work that is being done to address the needs of the dispossessed, many of whom are people of color. The social work profession can look back on its history as a force for social change in our society in which the beneficiaries were and are predominantly people of color.

Institutional racism is the manifestation of racism in social systems and institutions. It is the social, economic, educational, and political forces or policies that operate to foster discriminatory outcomes. It is the combination of polices, practices, or procedures embedded in bureaucratic structure that systematically lead to unequal outcomes for groups of people. In this environment disparities are often tolerated as normal rather than investigated and challenged. "These power-assigning social structures in the form of institutional racism affect the life opportunities, life-styles, and quality of life for both Whites and people-of-color. In so doing they compound, exaggerate, and distort biological and behavioral differences and reinforce misconceptions, myths, and distortions on the part of both groups about one another". In the United States, the ethnocentric focus is still primarily a white, Anglo-Saxon protestant orientation. The standards by which things are considered valued emanate from a Eurocentric perspective. Kivel noted the following examples of institutional racism over the history of this country:

— exclusions from unions, organisations, social clubs
— seniority systems (last hired, first fired)
— income differentials
— predatory lending practices
— inferior municipal services
— admissions based on test scores
— differential education based on preconceived potential or ability
— monocultural school curricula

In each of these situations, people of color experience disadvantages that flow from one generation to another in reference to income, decision making, health status, knowledge and skill development, and quality of life. The greater loss is to the country as a whole of the talents and perspectives of a significant proportion of the population.

Structural inequities have been solidified over time. The multigenerational effect of the privileges of free white people as compared with the effect of slavery, "Jim Crow" segregation, along with prejudicial immigration ruleshas resulted in a set of social structures that maintain and reinforce the barriers to the attainment of maximal human potential and dignity.

A strong social movement will be the most powerful approach to change. On the surface, this is a natural challenge for the social work profession to address. However, these social structures are maintained by individuals, many of whom are just trying to make a living. Their participation in these systems is not fueled by intention to do harm, and many are oblivious to the fact that anyone has been harmed. Some, including many social workers, believe that they are "doing good."

The new challenge for the profession is to tackle forms of racism that are more subtle than slavery or segregation. To a large degree, the social traditions and values within the helping professions preclude active promotion of the types of racism that are overt or blatant. Many in this society, including the helping professions, denounce intentional discrimination or prejudice against a person because of that person's membership in a certain racial group. The press for political correctness suppresses some behaviors or comments, and most people, including social workers or others in the helping professions, would not describe themselves as "racist." Nor do they engage in forms of overt racism. However, even if every person in the world currently conducted themselves in a non-racist manner, institutional racism would still exist.

These structures are maintained, in part, by individuals who exhibit some of the more subtle forms of racism that even they would not necessarily believe in themselves. The challenge for social workers committed to change is to address both overt forms of racism and these subtle forms as they are expressed by others and themselves.

Subtle Types of Racism

Three subtle types of racism are captured in the concepts of symbolic racism, aversive racism, and micro-inequities. Symbolic racism is expressed by those who may or may not perceive themselves as racist, but justify their negative judgment of others by asserting that the others do not abide by traditional values of the dominant group. People can perceive themselves as being fair and practicing equality by holding forth certain values, such as "individualism" or "work ethic" or "self-reliance," and take negative action because the focal group does not share those values. So they perceive themselves as operating based on certain "objective" standards or "universal truths" rather than in opposition to the group based on their race.

Aversive racism is another subtle form of prejudice. People who engage in the practice see themselves as non-racists, but they will do racist things, sometimes unintentionally, or they will avoid people without overt racist intent. What they believe about themselves and will attest to is the importance of fairness, equality, and justice, but because they have been exposed to the ever-present societal racism just by living in the United States, they will reflect it in their conduct. Finally, good people can do bad things to others in ways for which there is no formal grievance, but still have negative (sometimes unintentionally) effect. This refers to micro- aggressions or micro-inequities.

Micro-inequities are "those tiny, damaging characteristics of an environment, as these characteristics affect a person not of that environment. They are the comments, the work assignments, the tone of voice, the failure of acknowledgement in meetings or social gatherings. These are not actionable violations of law or policies, but they are clear, subtle indicators of lack of respect by virtue of membership in a group". These are forms of racism that as members of this society we all commit. People of color may commit these acts or maintain these attitudes against other people of color. The charge is to become able to recognise them and move ourselves and others beyond them to facilitate systemic change.

Two other issues must be confronted as a precondition to releasing the energy required to successfully challenge institutional racism. One is white privilege and the second is internalised racism. White privilege is the collection of benefits based on belonging to a group perceived to be white, when the same or similar benefits are denied to members of other groups. It is the benefit of access to resources and social rewards and the power to shape the norms and values of society that white people receive, unconsciously or consciously, by virtue of their skin color.

In contrast, internalised racism is the development of ideas, beliefs, actions, and behaviors that support or collude with racism against oneself. It is the support of the supremacy and dominance of the dominant group through participation in the set of attitudes, behaviors, social structures, and ideologies that undergirds the dominating group's power and privilege and limits the oppressed group's own advantages. The challenge for white social workers and social workers of color is to confront these inhibiting forces to the work required to successfully confront institutional racism.

Individuals are called upon to acknowledge that by the accident of history, they are in positions that give them advantages over others. And then, they are being asked to advocate for changes that may disadvantage themselves or their family members. Others are called upon to dare to recognise their own potential power, mourn the loss of what might have been, and marshal their energies to seek correction in society's processes. Even those within the social work profession can be paralysed against change because of benefits of white privilege or the blindness of internalised racism.

Racism and the Other Isms

Some people discount the effect of race on the outcomes for people of color. Many would argue that the issues for people of color are more a consequence of socioeconomic status than race. What they fail to recognise is that the overrepresentation of people of color in lower socioeconomic strata is due to institutional racism that has constrained them to life circumstances that kept them in that strata. Others equate the prejudice, discrimination, and bias based on age, gender, sexual orientation, or physical ability to the negative experiences due to race. Prejudice and discrimination based on these factors do in fact cause much strife in our society. Also, issues of privilege based on these factors must be confronted as seriously as privilege by racial identification. However, the experience of people of color in each of these categories is significantly worse compared with those who are white and in these categories. Furthermore, the intolerance that was first established on the basis of race provided the template to treat in a discriminatory manner those who do not "fit." If our society can successfully tackle its treatment of people who are "different" by virtue of the social category of race, it will have changed the manner in which it views, understands, and responds to "differentness" in other forms.

Institutional Racism in Social Work

Social work as a profession historically has had to confront two sometimes complementary and sometimes competing mandates. The preamble to the NASW Code of Ethics begins by stating:

> The primary mission of the social work profession is to enhance human well-being and help meet the basic human needs of all people, with particular attention to the needs and empowerment of people who are vulnerable, oppressed, and living in poverty.... Social workers are sensitive to cultural and ethnic diversity and strive to end discrimination, oppression, poverty, and other forms of social injustice.

The profession is expected to "enhance human well-being" and also "strive to end social injustice." The irony is that by being a "helping" profession, social work reduces the pressure on the larger society for social change. The continued marginalisation of those who should or could be mobilised to act for social justice could be an unintended consequence of the profession's "helpfulness." The other dilemma is that success in changing the forces that promote discrimination, oppression, and poverty also changes the forces that support white privilege. NASW as a predominantly white association must acknowledge and commit to taking action against white privilege, if it is to be successful in achieving social justice for people of color.

A Self-Assessment of the Profession

A thoughtful examination of the practice in the association, in social work organisations, in institutions, in agencies, and by individual social work practitioners would probably reveal examples of different subtle forms of racism. If the profession can understand the manifestation of the different forms of racism within the profession, it can gain a better understanding of the issues, discover strategies that work for change, and become authentic social change leaders against structural racism in a variety of societal institutions. Consider the following familiar scenarios:

Support is given to policies and practices without analysis of the racial effect or worse.

Scenario A. A program designed to reduce disproportionate confinement of youths of color in juvenile detention settings reviewed its decision-making policies. It discovered that one assessment question was sending children of color into detention with greater frequency than white children. The question was "Is there a parent available for supervision immediately after school?" In this community, most of the families of color were single-family units, in which the parent was at work immediately after school. When the question was changed to "Is there a responsible adult available for supervision immediately after school?", the disposition patterns of that community changed.

Scenario B. A senior social worker of color, employed by a state agency to monitor mental health programs, finds that assessments of black families and children do not adequately consider the social context and family strengths. When she raises such concerns with white program leaders, she is frequently told that she is missing the clinical aspects of what is involved, even though she is an experienced clinician, herself.

Board leadership and membership and executive leadership and management positions are occupied predominantly by white people, even in institutions that serve predominantly populations of color

Scenario C. City X's population is 40% multicultural. The service community is 80% African American or Caribbean American. The three primary social service agencies providing services in this community have boards that are 100% white. The executive directors are white. The senior management positions are white. The front line service staff is 30% multicultural. The administrative clerks and housekeeping staff are 80% multicultural.

Scenario D. A Vietnamese social work administrator is recruited into a large family service agency to help the organisation move toward becoming more diverse and multicultural. She soon finds that she is expected to address issues of diversity without the executive leadership and board members assuming greater responsibility, themselves. She finds it very difficult to express her concerns about this out of a realistic fear of being told that she is too sensitive.

Organisations that are led by people of color are marginalised by organisations led by members of the dominant society

Scenario E. In community Y, four social service agencies provide most of the services. A consortium of African

American, Cuban, Haitian, and Puerto Rican–led community-based social service agencies wants to expand their services. The leaders of the four dominant social service agencies refuse to engage in dialogue with the consortium about partnerships. The state agency promulgates rules in the request for proposal that advantage the established agencies and disadvantages the consortium. Unless there is change these agencies will not have the opportunity to demonstrate whether they can effectively provide the appropriate services to the community. And in the current fiscal environment, they may not be able to survive as service providers.

Investment in the development of knowledge about people and communities of color is limited.

Scenario F. State Z mandates that child welfare agencies engage in cultural and linguistic competence training. The agencies in this particular city conduct annual cultural competence training consisting of an eight-hour training session providing an overview of cultural competence and stories from four members of the community about their culture. Staff members who have been there for several years are bored after hearing the same presentation year after year. No other training is provided. Staff members are not expected to develop a personal professional development plan in relationship to cultural competence. There is no programmatic effort to link with the various cultural communities on an ongoing basis.

Scenario G. A coalition of agencies approaches a school of social work to urge that curriculum better reflect the needs of the Latino community. The school's dean says that she agrees with the request but the faculty has a great deal of discretion in determining the curriculum. She did not feel she was in a position to insist on implementation of the requested changes.

Scenario H. A social worker of color who runs a program for children in foster care shared an experience in which a white clinician reported to him that an African American child's grandmother, who was the primary caregiver, was resistant to working with the agency after she had missed several appointments. The program director said that when he looked more closely at the situation, he found that the grandmother was caring for three of the child's siblings, including one who had recently required hospitalisation. Instead of seeing her as resistant, he found her to be a significant asset to the child, but overextended and stressed. He concluded that the clinician did not understand the commitment of many African American families in assuming responsibility for children even when they are not the biological parents.

There is limited investment in creating partnerships with communities of color for program or service design, implementation, and evaluation

Scenario I. In response to the need to provide better aging services in rural communities, this social service agency has decided to expand services from its base in the major city in this southern community to satellite offices in the rural communities contiguous to the city. The executive director and management staff of the agency developed a service delivery structure after consultation with a wellrespected consultant in the field. Like other social service agencies, the service population in both the city and the rural communities are predominantly African American, along with an influx of immigrants from Mexico, El Salvador and Guatemala but the board and executive directors are white. Part of the process included meetings with physicians and religious leaders in the rural area. Prospective consumers of the services or their families were not involved in the planning, design, or implementation. They were asked to complete a satisfaction survey at the end of service, but they had no input into the questions or analysis of the results.

Scenario J. In an effort to make family and children's services neighborhood based, a public child welfare agency awarded contracts to several established white-run nonprofit organisations with little history in the communities they were coming into. Whereas one community-based agency had a long-standing reputation for its involvement with the public schools, hospitals, police precinct, and cultural institutions in its neighborhood, the other contracted providers made little effort to develop such relationships.

There is preference to soften racist language so that one sees euphemisms such as, "culturally deprived" and "economically disadvantaged" rather than "culturally dispossessed" and "economically exploited"

Scenario K. In a study being developed as background for a state legislative committee, this policy analysis group notes significant racial disparities in mental health services for the African Americans in one particular region of the state. It is a community that has received numerous complaints regarding racial profiling by police, predatory lending practices, and cross burnings. Rather than explore and discuss racism as a potential factor, they focus on the cultural orientation of the residents to use faith communities as a source of healing. They shift the focus to the residents rather than the institutions and policies.

Social workers of color experience micro-inequities promulgated by their white social work colleagues.

Scenario L. In recent interviews with social workers of color in a major city about their experiencing bias among colleagues toward them, several reported, independently of one another, having their perspectives and concerns treated as unimportant. Significantly, all of them said that they also experienced having the same perspectives and concerns valued when expressed by a white person. One black program director said that he repeatedly reported that an air conditioning unit in a room where groups were run was broken during a hot summer, but it was not repaired until another administrator, who was white, made the report.

Employment criteria and credentialing requirements often create barriers for employment of social workers of color and generally do not require demonstration of the knowledge and skills required to effectively serve a culturally and linguistically diverse service population.

Scenario M. Native American social workers in County A have consistently found it difficult to meet the criteria of the social work regulatory body in their state. As they pursue tutoring in preparation for the test, they are amased at how few test items seem to relate to the issues and needs of tribal communities or best practices with this population. They despair that they are having a hard time meeting the formal criteria of the state and of obtaining social work positions to serve their community, while at the same time, the state credentialing body is not setting forth an expectation that those who are credentialed are prepared to serve their tribal community.

Scenario N. A hospital social work director terminated the employment of four social workers because they did not comply with a policy requiring all staff to pass the state's licensing exam within one year of being hired. Each social worker had been highly evaluated. For three social workers, Spanish, Hmong, and Vietnamese were their primary languages and English was their second language. The fourth social worker, an African American, grew up in an inner-city neighborhood where the quality of education was inferior to that of more affluent areas. This resulted in lower test scores throughout her life. The director said that this was a significant loss to the department and hospital, which was in a low-income and immigrant community.

Each of these examples demonstrates the ripple effect of institutional or structural racism in our society into social work practice. The correction in each of these circumstances requires authentic efforts to name "racism" as a factor for exploration and action. The journey to effective transformation is not straightforward. The following section maps out strategies to address these issues within the profession.

INSTITUTIONAL RACISM IN THE SOCIAL WORK PROFESSION

The approaches to address institutional racism in the social work profession discussed here are not necessarily comprehensive in scope but identify some significant dimensions, including short- and long-term approaches. Strategies geared toward different levels of social organisation are also needed, starting at the level of the individual professional social worker, moving to the level of social work organisations and then to social institutions that impinge on the profession and on clients and their communities. Addressing these levels are not mutually exclusive but are intertwined; they are separated out here to bring attention to the importance of each level.

Long-Term Approaches

Personal Growth and Professional Development

All social workers need to dedicate time to their personal growth and professional development to become and remain effective in addressing institutional racism. Whereas social workers are likely to fall along a continuum from having little professional development to being knowledgeable and effective in this area, growth and development is an ongoing process of continuous learning throughout one's career.

Multiple elements contribute to personal growth and professional development, beginning with the recognition of the importance of institutional racism as a variable in social work and the lives of clients and the communities in which they live. Coupled with this awareness is the need to make a commitment to acquire the knowledge and skills necessary to be both competent and effective.

Interpersonal Capacity and Collaboration

Social workers have limited capacity to address institutional racism on their own. Although individuals must assume responsibility for their own growth and development, it is essential for professional social workers to initiate discussions, both formal and informal, about the issues discussed here, with colleagues and members of the organisations within which they work. The conversations need to take place both as general discussions and in response to specific policies, practices, behaviors, and attitudes observed or planned in their professional context. This is often easier said than done, given the nature of institutional racism and that discussion is often experienced as threatening. Becoming skilled in initiating and maintaining discussions about institutional racism requires critical judgment, skill, and self-awareness that evolve over time.

Social work organisations becoming antiracist entities

Social work and social work–related organisations include agencies, programs, and departments that provide social work services; schools of social work; and associations such as the National Association of Social Workers (NASW) and the Council on Social Work

Education (CSWE). Organisations need to move from remaining silent about, or ignoring, the manifestations of institutional racism to recognising their existence and making a commitment to promote change.

This movement begins with the individual members of the organisation engaging in their own professional development and growth while entering into interpersonal collaborations with colleagues and other members of the organisation. It is essential, however, for organisational decision makers to assume leadership for addressing institutional racism and developing official goals, policies, and procedures that will enable the organisation to evolve. In organisations engaged in service delivery this effort will include a commitment by boards of directors and ongoing analysis of how institutional racism can be ameliorated or reversed through programming, hiring, training, supervision, and other forms of institutional processes.

In educational institutions, effectiveness in addressing institutional racism will involve making a commitment to the incorporation of content related to institutional racism into curriculum and all forms of education. The goal is to graduate social workers who are on the road toward competency in addressing institutional racism throughout their careers. It also means examining ways in which the current curriculum promotes and supports values, beliefs, and practices that foster institutional racism and then engaging in change process as indicated. Leadership is needed from deans and directors, chairs of educational committees, as well as from admissions and field work departments and field work supervisors.

Focus on Client, Community, and Social Policy

Fundamental to addressing institutional racism is the need for professional social workers and social work–

related organisations to understand the effect of racism on their clients and their communities. There is a need to better understand the relationship between the problems a client needs help with and the role of racism in the genesis of those problems, regardless of the race or socioeconomic status of the client. Social workers need to adapt their own practice approach in consideration of these factors. Social workers also need to be attuned to the differential effect of social policies that disadvantage communities of color while benefiting others, and advocate for fairness and equity in policy decision and resource distribution.

Society cannot be changed overnight. However,

- Social workers can assume responsibility for taking action to reverse the effect of racism on services to people and communities of color.
- Social workers can take action to engage their own organisations to become antiracist organisations.
- Social workers can partake in actions large and small to challenge the institutional or structural racism in their communities and the nation at large.

Both individual initiatives and collective organised efforts officially endorsed by social work organisations are required to make this happen. Opportunities for leadership also reside with schools of social work and social work service delivery organisations. Social work leaders, from CEOs and program directors to members of boards of directors, have a special obligation to address institutional racism and can do so, given their sphere of influence and ability to influence organisational decisions and structures.

The following opportunities can be taken immediately while building toward longer term and ongoing efforts:

Recognition/Create awareness. Efforts to address institutional racism begin with recognition of the dimensions of the problem and how it is manifested within the social work profession. It is especially critical to recognise how institutional racism is ignored through a process of denial. Only through recognition and building awareness can a commitment be made to create short- and long-term plans for institutionalising positive change.

5

Social Work Strategies for Human Rights Protection

Human rights allow us to the loss of morality. Morality is the safe guard of human rights. Social work develops the humanity, honesty and responsibility in mankind for differentiating a man form an animal by growing the moral value to the individuals. For the protection of human rights, social work promoted programs all over the world through the Bill of Rights, Covenants & Conventions. Thus social justice takes place in the society of the global village. National & International organizations plays a crucial role for the observance of human rights.

Human Rights is a sensitive subject the study of which is full of pitfalls. It is the cornerstone of peace and security for all nations and it is universally acknowledged as it has special importance in the fabric of international relations. It is clear that the concept of human rights is the most ancient though its origination is uncertain. It is realized that word human rights was originated from the first written epic of the world.

Every major human civilization underwent a process of transformation in which it felt the dignity of human beings at its heart. The contemporary world is also under going a phase of noticeable change toward the direction of achieving the basic rights of mankind and narrowing the gap between the poor and the rich communities. As a matter of fact, the end of 20th century is experiencing a series of social, economic and political struggle across the world to earn self dependence and self respect from the rule of oppression.

Globally, the 20th century people are asserting that every society is entitled as a matter of legal right to have his or her dignity and freedoms respected and his or her basic needs satisfied which is why it is thought that recognition promotion and protection of human rights is a product of the present time. A new era of human night and political freedom seemed to be dawning as the world has entered into the 21st century. At the national and regional levels also human rights has been discussed with crucial importance all over the world.

Despite this man has a special quality of his own. The growth and development of these qualities and existence can ensure the amelioration of both individual and groups, this is why suitable environment and affluent facilities are necessary for them. Generally, Rights means the ability of living or doing something by one's own wish.

Harold. J. Laski observed " Rights are those conditions of social life without which no man can seek in general, to be himself at his best" Hobhouse viewed rights thus "Rights are what we expect from others and others from us and all genuine rights are conditions of social welfare. Finally it can be said that, Rights are such achieved facilities by which man can preserve his own facilities in a confessed way by the state, society or constitution.

The word Human Rights has been sprung up from the English translation of the French declaration of the right of man and the citizen by thomas Raine in 1789. But its origin is prolonged and the evolution of human Rights is also prolonged as it has a central role in the life of a nation and its citizens. Human Rights allow us to develop our human qualities, intelligence, talents and conscience. It also helps to satisfy our spiritual and other needs.

Human Rights have gradually evolved over the years and are based on mankind's increasing demand for a life in which the inherent dignity and worth of human being will receive respect and protection. In the Journal on "Teaching human rights of U.N. in 1989, Human Rights is defined thus, "Human Rights could be generally defined, as those right which are inherent in our nature and without which we can not live as human beings".

According to Jacques Maritain "The human person posses rights because of the very fact that it is a person, a whole, a master of itself and its act, and which consequently is not merely a means to an end, but an end, which must be treated as such". As " Manobong Aumritasya Putraa." so human rights are those rights with which human beings born and get extra-ordinary and become beast when they lose these rights.We may discuss human rights into two dimensions: (1) Natural Rights (ii) Positive Rights At the dawn of civilization when man lived indiscriminately, No

Rights was confessed by them but afterwards when they tried to be civilized, they became aware of their rights. Meanwhile, this thinking has been veering round the theory that man has certain inherent, inalienable immutable and involute freedoms and rights which nobody on earth could take away. It was asserted that the state was bound to recognize these rights and freedom and allow them a free play. Thus there emerged a new thesis on fundamental rights based on the philosophy of natural law.

The concept of natural law which pronounced the new philosophy of law asserted that the positive law out to be subordinated to the natural law. It was proclaimed how is an expression of the will of the community. Notwithstanding it can be said that positive rights are such rights which are issued for the establishment of natural rights as these are violated. Besides positive rights support the natural rights. So it is beyond speaking that Human Rights are the aggregate feature of Natural Rights and positive Rights.

Philosophy of Human Rights

Anything without philosophy would be drab or dreary and everything of philosophy is always free from bleak and bleary. As philosophy is the thoughts, sense, doctrine of a particular thing, even the values, characteristics, principles, all are included in philosophy. Any theory of philosophical thought is derived from the light of sense of doctrine. Just as human rights is the bright lamp to levee the rights of mankind.

The thought and philosophy of human rights was based on the betterment of humanity and social amelioration. Viewing the welfare of the society the philosophers and thinkers of Egypt Babylon, Greece, Jebulistan, China and India played a crucial role for the establishment of human rights.

In the days of yore, when man did not know what their rights & duties are and were all going to misled, in the meantime they were instructed by the divine power and messengers were sent to them and thus they tried to live on the boundary of Dharma. "Dharma is that which sustains and ensures progress us and welfare of all; in this world and eternal bless in the other world". "Dharma is what holds together or a code of duties for the harmonious functioning of the various divisions of society, the inculcation of the spirit of Dharma shall provide high standing of ethics, clear cut codes of behavior and a widespread acceptance of nonmaterial values as of higher importance than possessions, have come to be the expression in ordinary society.

It is worth while to note that all the oriental doctrines emphasize human rights. One of the reasons is that these doctrines were laid down by the prophets and their disciples who urged the people to live together in a compact society to implement the will of God. We find an interesting coincidence in human rights thinking among the Semitic Hebrews and the Aryan Hindus.

The Hindus believed that poverty fallen upon a man, was due to his mischievous activities in his former life. Instructions have been issued to be kind to the poor and needy. These laws were propagated by the religious leaders. The Hebrew or Judaic details are contained in the Mosaic law. The commands of Moses are the basis of their laws. All the spheres of life had been put under the laws which include equal footing. Moral values were important basis for social and economic laws. In the Hebrew it is said in respect of Hunan Rights:

> "Do not forget to do good and to help to one another, because these are the sacrifices that please God".

Human Rights and the Grecian Social thought

We may expect to find, therefore, in Grecian social thought important new contributions which are complementary to the legacies from the He brews, and which, when taken in conjunction with Chinese social thought and with the early Christenian forms of Hebrew social thought constitute the main foundations of modern social thought regarding Human Rights.

At the dawn of the ninth century B.C Lycurgus declared that the state owned the child and urged a system of education which would prepare the child fit for the state. The influence of the sophist leaders, such as *Protagoras, Gorgas, Callicles, Thrasymachus* brought forward the problem of training pupils to solve civic questions. Their philosophy was "Man is the measure of all things." based on the thought of Concord, Moderation or Harmony and "what is best for the individual is best for the society".

Socratic thought: Socrates (469-399 B.C) asserted that the qualities of justice, wisdom, temperance, and courage which make an individual a good member of society and which increase social welfare. His Philosophy was "Virtue is knowledge, wishing to make all men intelligent.

Plato (427-347 B.C.): " Plato stated that God created the individual for the whole not the whole for the individual so worship to God is necessary to prevent him reverting from swinishness of character".

Aristotle (384-322): He said the coward is he who avoids and fears anything ; the foolhardy is he who rushes into danger anywhere.. Virtue it self is the mean between self-indulgence and asceticism. On the light of "primacy of law", he preferred the citizen in expressing opinion and added (i) To establish the right of the lower class citizen. (ii) Coherence between the government and the citizen. (iii) Equality in individual and class. (iv) Prohibition on suppression and deprivation.

He said that the protection of human rights would never be possible if there were no protection of the right of the disregarded. *Epicurus* (342-270 B.C.) Self sacrifice and noble conduct in the social sense are foreign to *Eqicureanism.* "Friends should be sought not for the sake of cultivating their friendship, but for the pleasure of the seeker". *Stoicism,* founded by *Zeno,* culmination among the Romans, *Poly bius* stated that people associated because of the selfish benefits that accrue.

Roman thought and Human Rights

Roman thought was rich in the explanation of law: (i)Jus civile, (ii) Jus gentium, (iii) Jus nalure.

Seneca (4 B.C.-65 A.D) "Benevolence is the most social of all virtues and the ingratitude is the most venal of all crimes". "Proper giving is very difficult. It must be just and reasonable, causes of proper giving may be; (i) to do a survival (ii) to make a return (iii) to give succour, (iv) to give a deserving person from being dragged doers by poverty. (v) to those needy whose pride keeps them away from asking *Marcur Auselius* (121-180 Ad.) "This is a social world; men exist for the sake of one another." *Epetetus* (60-120 A.D.) "you ought to pity one who is offensive".

"Much property is burden and causes of worry and fear it excites envy in others". So help the destitute by all your means. Infact religion is the basis of Human Rights as well as social welfare. Religious sentiment drives people to engage themselves for the betterment of humanity. The charter of human rights was come from religion and the Universal Declaration of Human Rights is the codification and modification of the given rights of the latest and sophisticated religion.

Christianism and Human Rights

"Service to humanity is better to the Almighty". Christianism is based on this truth which is a part and parcel of human rights.

Now we may see what is said in this religion.

"Never tell your neighbor to wait until tomorrow if you can help him now"

"Happy are those who are merciful to others, God will be merciful to them". (Mathw-5:7)

"When some one asks for some thing give it to him, when some one wants to borrow some thing, lend it to him". (Mathew 5:42) "God will judge you in the same way as you judge others and he will apply to you the same rule you apply to others". (Mathew-7:2)

"The lord says, I love justice and hate oppression and crime", (Isaiah 61:8)

"Do not take revenge on some one who wrongs you . It anyone slaps you on the right cheek, let him slap your left cheek too".(Mathew 5:38)

If your enemy is hungry, feed him, if he is thirsty give him a drink".(Isaiah 35:6)

Human Rights and Islam

It is Islam which gave the security of all rights of mankind. Truly the original philosophy of human rights has been originated from Islamic thought Islam extended the ambit of Human Rights and brought wholeness in it in all side in need. Now we may state the Quranic thought in respect of Human Rights.

(i) Right to life and liberty.

"And do not kill yourselves " (nor kill one another) Quran 4:29

"And do not kill anyone whose killing Allah has forbidden, Quran 17:33

The Prophet said- "Your life, property and status all are secred and transgressless". He who commits suicide by throtting shall keep on throtting himself in the Hell fire (forever), and he who commits suicide by stabbing himself shall keep on stabbing in the Hell fire (forever) "Bukhari 2: 445.

(ii) Right to equality and non discrimination:

"O Mankind, we have created you from a male and

female, and made you into nations and tribes that you may know one another. Quran 49:13.

(iii) Right to property:

"O mankind who believe! "Eat not up your property among yourselves unjustly". Quran 4:29

(iv) Freedom of movements:

"He it is who has made the earth subservient to you., so walk in the path there of". Quran 67:15

(v) Right against arbitrary arrest:

Imam Maleque said- " No man can be imprisoned without justice".

(vi) Freedom of thought and expression:

"The believers men and women are helpers, supporters, friends, protectors of one another". Quran 9:7. (vii) Right to privacy: "O you who believe ; Enter not houses other than your own, until you have asked permission agreed those in them". Quran 24:27.

"O you who believe: avoid much suspicion, indeed some suspicions are sins and spy not". 49:12 Narrated Hudhaifah , I heard prophet (SM) saying.

"A Qattat (spyee) will not enter paradise. "Bukhari 8:82

(viii) Right to take part in public affairs:

So pass over their faults and ask forgiveness for then and consult them in the affairs, Quran.3:

(ix) Right against slavery:

"The best way to get the love of lord and ownership of Heaven is to free a slave who is black and distress."

(x) Right to marry and Right to family.

"And marry those among you who are single and the pious, fit and capable ones" Quran 24:32 Besides Islam gave all the nights that belonged in human rights we may include some other:

Right to nationality, Cultural rights, freedom of conscience and religion Right to work, Right to social security, cultural rights, freedom of conscience and religion, Right to work, Right to protection to moral and melerial interest Right to minimum standard of living. Finally we may state our prophet's words that is a declaration of human rights, "He is not a true Muslim who eats his fill when his next door neighbor is hungry" Bukhari.

Protection and Implementation of Human Rights

The ongoing journey of Human Rights was started at the dawn of civilization and has been moving ceaselessly till today for the eradication of economic exploitation and psycho-physiological suppression. Some times the moral value of Human Rights has been trod down by the social beings the cause behind is the loss of moral values. "Morality is the safeguard of Human Rights".

For the protection of Human Rights many steps were taken, these are adornable and hugged by the society as thereby rights of mankind has been established the Petition of Rights in England Stated the following rights freedom from Marshal law, Right to vote, Rescue from the illegal hand over, individual privacy and residence, freedom from illegal arrest. The Puriterian revolution of England 1649 caused the class struggle in a world oppressor and oppressed and then the following rights were included: Right to acquisition of wealth and enjoyment, right to vote and right to news paper.

Then the English Bill of Rights included: Right to free election. freedom of speech and expression, Right to bail, just of jurisprudence, escape of unexpected punishment. In the charter of U.S. Declaration of independence. The Declaration of the Rights of man and the citizen was written for the first time and laid down in several domestic constitutions particularly those of the France in.

Many Constitutions of the world noted Human Rights as "Bill of Rights". The France Declaration included- Right to Life, Freedom, Property and security, where as Rousseau proclaimed that man were endowed with in alienable rights of liberty , equality and fraternity. In 1929 the institute of international low adopted a declaration of International Right of man. With rise the fascism in Germany and Italy and the out break of world war 11 the question of fundamental rights of man became much more important and loomed large in many international deliberations and covenants. Joint Declaration of the US. President Roosevelt, and Great Britain's Prime Minister Churchill, the Atlantic Charter of August 1941 where in it was proclaimed that " To see established a peace which will afford to all nations of dwelling in safety within their own boundaries and which will afford assurance that all men in all the lands may live out their lives in freedom from fear and want". Then the United Nations Declaration of January 1,1942 put on record that complete victory over their enemies is essential to defend life liberty independence and religious freedoms and to preserve human rights and justice in their own lands as well as in other lands.

The Big Three endorsed the above declaration in their conference of March 3,1943. Then came the Philadelphia Declaration of the International Labor Organizations 26th Session which laid down: All human beings irrespective of trade, creed or sex have the right to pursue both their material wellbeing and their spiritual development in conditions of freedom and dignity of economic security and equal opportunity". The Dumbarton Oaks Conference of 1944 among the four big powers led to the first tentative draft of a New World Organization. Here it was proclaimed "Facilities solutions of international economic, social, and other humanitarian problems and promote respect for human rights and fundamental rights." Then came on April 95, 1945 the Sanfrancisco Conference of the United Nations where the charter U.N emerged.

Human Rights were expressed in pious terms in treaties Prior to coming into force of the U.N Charter, human rights movement was confined to abolition of slavery, humaniterianlaws of welfare and protection of minorities. Obviously, it was imperative for the world organization to take stock of ground realities and create some mechanism for the protection of human rights. Human Rights has been pronounced in the article 55 & 56 of the U.N. charter. "With a view to the creation of conditions of stability and wellbeing which are necessary for peaceful and friendly relations among nations based on respect for the principle of equal rights and self determination of peoples, the U.N, shall promote Universal respect for and observance of human rights and fundamental freedoms for all without distinction as to race, sex, language or religion "Article 55. And Human Rights is stated in the articles 1(iii), 13(i)/B, 55© , 62 (ii) and 76 (c) of the U.N charter, Besides it is stated too by Marshal smooth on the preface of the U.N. Charter.

As the U.N. charter is an international contact so through the principle of good faith in treaty interpretation it can be said that the members are bound to protect and implement human rights by signing it. In 26 June 1945 signing of the charter of the U.N. and the statute of the International court of justice in San Francisco.

In 21 June 1946 the ECOSOC established the commission on Human Rights and the commission on the status of Women, Then 10 Dec. 48, The General Assembly adopted the Universal Declaration of Human Rights. In respect of this Mrs. Roosevelt the chairperson of Human Rights commission stated, "The Declaration was not a treaty or international agreement and did not impose legal obligation, it was rather a statement of principles of inalienable human rights setting up a common standard of achievement for all peoples, all nations"

Then 20 Dec 52 the Convention on the political Right of Woman 1 Aug 56, ECOSOC calls for periodic reports on human rights and studies of specific rights or groups of rights. 21 Dec 65. International commission on the Elimination of all forms of Racial Discrimination. In 16 Dec.66. The International covenant on Economic Social and Cultural Rights and the International Covenant on Civil and Political Rights. This is for the implementation of Human Rights.

Civil and Political Rights:

i) Right to equality and non-discrimination (7)

ii) Right to life and liberty (3.7 of the U.D. H.R)

(iii) Right against Arbitrary arrest (9,10/ I)

(iv) Right against self incrimination

(v) Freedom of movements.

(vi) Freedom of thoughts and expression

(vii) Right to assemble peacefully

(viii) Right to property

(ix) Freedom of conscience of Religion

(x) Right against slavery

(xi) Right to privacy

(xii) Right to marry and Right to family

(xiii) Right to nationality

(xiv) Equal access to public services

(xv) Right to take part in public affairs

(xvi) Right to form association.

(xvii) Cultural rights

(xviii) Right to minorities

Economic social and cultural rights

(i) Right to work,

(ii) Right to Social Security.

(iii) Right to equal pay for equal work.

(iv) Right to leisure

(v) Right to protection of Mother hood and Child hood.

(vi) Right to education.

(vii) Right to protection of moral and material interest.

(viii) Right to strike

(ix) Right to trade unions

(x) Right to maternity benefits.

(xi) Right to minimum standard of livings.

Finally we can state the article 1 where in "All people and all nations, have the right of self determination. By virtue of that right they freely determine their economic, social and cultural Rights. The proclamation of Tehran in 1968 impressed "Since human rights and fundamental freedoms are indivisible the full realization of civil and political rights with out the enjoyment of economic social and cultural rights is impossible. The achievement of lasting progress in the implementation of human rights is dependent upon sound and effective national and international development policies economic and social development.

In 30 Nov. 73, International Convention on the Suppression and Punishment of the Crime of Apartheid 9 Dec. 75, Declaration on the protection of All persons from being subjected to torture and other cruel inhuman or degrading treatment or punishment. 25 Nove.81 The Convention on the Elimination of All Forms of Discrimination and of Intolerance based on Religion or Belief.

9 Dec. 1988 the Body of Principles for the protection of All persons under any form of Detention or Imprisonment.

18 Dec 90, The International Convention on the protection of the Right of all Migrant Workers and Members of their Families. 18, Dec. 92. Declaration on the Rights of Persons Belong to National or Ethnic, Religious and linguistic Minorities, 20 Dec. 93 establishing post of United Nations High Commissioner for Human Rights. 23 Dec, 94 The General Assembly proclaims the UN. Decade for Human Rights Education.17 July 98 Rome Statute of the International Criminal Court; establishing the International Criminal Court.

The European system for protecting Human Rights; It is Primarily composed of two major treaties; The European convention on Human Rights and Fundamental Freedoms (ECHR) and the European social charter (ESC). The ECHR which was focused upon the protection of civil and political rights was adopted in 1950 and entered into force in 1953.

The ECHR and its ten additional protocols protect most of the rights contained in the Universal Declaration

ECHR Enforcement Mechanism

Inter state complaints it's applications, however, trend out as being motivated not by political hostility but by genuine humanitarian concerns. These are the cases brought by Denmark, Norway, Sweden, and the Netherlands against Greece in 1970 and by the same states against turkey in 1982. Besides the European convention for the prevention of Torture and Inhuman or degrading treatment or punishment 1987 is also a preventative mechanism.

The Inter American system for protecting Human Rights: It has evolved within the frame work of the organizations of American states (OAS) 1948. The inter American human rights system is distinctive as it has its origin in two separate but substantially interrelated legal instruments.

Additional protocol by becoming parties to those instruments, American commission on Human Rights and the Charter system, that is promotional, advisory and consultative and protective.

The African system For protecting Human and Peoples Rights: The African charter, Sometimes known as the Banjul Charter after the Capital of the Gambia where it was drafted is the most recent of the regional human rights instruments to come in to force. It was adopted at the Eighteenth Assembly of Heads of state and government of the Organization of African Unity (OAU) in Nairobi, in June 81 and entered into force on 21 Oct. 1986. It might also be argued that of all the regional instruments, the African charter faces the most acute challenges. The holistic approach to human rights is prefaced by the preamble to the charter, which states .... that it is henceforth essential to pay particular attend to the right to development and that civil and political rights cannot be dissociated from economic, social and cultural rights.

Human rights are part of contemporary political and legal discourse at both national and international level. In Manila Regional council on Human Rights in Asia 18 Feb.

1982 was formed for the regional Human Rights Protection in Asia then the Declaration of the Basic duties of Asian peoples and governments has been expressed in Indonesia.

Casual perusal of number of U.N. and NGO reports on action in the field of human rights none the use bear testimony to the fact that despite the exponential growth in human rights instruments and institutions since the end of the second world war there are still widespread violations of human rights in many parts of the wold Nevertheless the Human Rights commission, the sub-commission on prevention of Discrimination and protection of Minorities, Working groups and Human Rights committee also doing their best to accelerate the pace of human right's observance.

Professionals in Protecting and Promoting Human Rights

It is very encouraging that professionals have shown increasing interest in matters relating to human rights. As awareness on human rights increases, more and more professional groups are joining the movement to uphold them and resist their violation. Doctors with their skills of forensic testing are now joining hands with activists and lawyers to develop methods of verifying incidence of assault rape etc. Women entrepreneurs are coming forward with ideas and resources as never before, Well – known artists have lent their voices and talents to inform, to communicate and to sensitize.

Journalists and the print media continuously bring the issues to national attention and are collaborating with affected groups. There is a realization amongst various professional groups that street activism has to join hands and run parallel with professional knowledge, commitment of the elite, and mass mobilization of the elite, and mass mobilization f people from all walks of life is needed in order to make a dent on human rights in general and violence against women in particular. From this realization sprang organizations like Coordinating Council for Human Rights.

But there is a general lack of such organizations specifically dedicated to human rights at the grassroots level. Like those at the national level, professionals working at lower levels can also play a constructive role in protecting and promoting human rights, particularly for the downtrodden. The professional forums formed locally in different parts of the country under the auspices of different NGOs have demonstrated considerable success in the area of human rights.

The legal Education and Support Service (LESS), a project of RDRS, though of somewhat different type, has shown promising results in women's empowerment process in general and in their legal rights in particular. Likewise the Human Rights Imporovement Societies formed in some districts are doing commendable jobs in the way of helping the poor through arbitration and mediation. Their success, whatever limited it might be has led to the hypothesis that self-sustained, spontaneously formed local bodies, not the ones imposed from outside, will be more effective in protecting and promoting human rights at the grassroots level. Local professionals, Particularly lawyers, doctors, journalists, teachers and social workers have a clear role to play in this regard.

Lawyers

It is the lawyers who can create awareness by educating the people about the fundamental human rights available in international instruments as well in the national constitution and legal documents. Being trained in the field, they can possibly do better than anyone else, in making people aware of the rights and privileges to which they are entitled. They must actively engage them for simple reason that unless a case involving breach of human rights is brought before court hardly it is possible for the judge to mend such breach suo moto.

Journalists

The media and journalists can play a very important role in creating mass awareness about district level legal aid committees and other bodies / associations which are available locally to provide assistance in legal matters. Also it is the journalists who through their reporting and investigative approach, can constantly keep public informed of the current human rights situation and thus help from strong pressure groups. Indeed, it is they who bring the notice of official bodies-mummeries facts, abuses, gaps and violations of human rights. an honest journalist is no less than a social worker.

Social Workers

Social and human rights workers are already doing good job in various spheres including the promotion of human rights. Their efforts have been found to be complementing the activities of government and NGOs in their crusade against poverty and exploitation. What is needed today is a campaign of education to put human face on human rights to identify the rights of starving people, those who lose their land unjustly, those whose children are kidnapped for immoral purposes, those who are mistreated because their families are too poor to give dowry and all those who suffer injustice because they have no one to help them.

The social workers can take a lead in this campaign, They can engage further in preventive and rehabilitative work for those who are or may become victims of human rights violation and exploitation of any kind. The future may also hold the Islamic world and perhaps even the south-east Asian and south pacific areas. What one can say with some certainty, however, is that human rights will continue to be a central part of the international agenda in the Twenty first century.

6

Social Work for Immigrants and Refugees

The worldwide movement of people is also an expression of globalisation that is particularly relevant for social work. Throughout history, policies on immigrants and refugees have been influenced by the competing values and themes of humanitarian response, human rights, security, and economics. At different points, one or more of these themes has gained ascendancy and brought about changes in immigration laws, affecting the lives of those within and outside the borders of the United States.

The profession of social work is concerned with immigration and refugee policies because many of our clients are affected by these policies and practices either directly or indirectly. In addition, immigration and refugee policies concern issues of social justice and human rights, issues that are at the heart of the social work profession. As expressed by Edith Abbott in a call for more social service involvement in migration research: "(migration) includes large questions of public policy, involving issues of national prosperity and human rights".

Although the United States defines itself as a country of immigrants, the degree of openness to immigration has varied considerably throughout history.

The immigrant population of the country increased significantly during the 1990s and early years of the 21st century. More than one in every nine inhabitants of the United States is an immigrant, 11.5 percent of the population. This is the highest percentage since 1930 and up dramatically from the low of 5 percent in 1970. If the current rate of immigration continues, the percentage of foreign-born people in the population by the year 2050 will equal the all-time high of 15 percent reached in 1900. Already, one in every five school children is the child of immigrants as are one of four low income children in the United States, and one half of all new workers entering the U.S. workforce in the 1990s were immigrants. Therefore, it is hard to overstate the significance of immigration and immigration policy.

Migration has affected many other countries during the same time period, turning previously homogeneous countries into multicultural ones and further diversifying the populations of already heterogeneous nations. Although the United States accepts a significant number of refugees for permanent resettlement and more immigrants on a citizenship track than other countries, it is important to recognise migration as a global phenomenon that plays a significant role in macro economic and political stability of sending as well as receiving countries. In fact, most of the world's refugees are either displaced within their own borders or have fled to neighboring countries where they pose a burden on struggling economies.

Immigration Law and Policies

The history of immigration laws and policies in the United States reflects the search for balance between humanitarianism and exclusion and alternatively has emphasized welcome, ambivalence, and fear of immigrants. This is clearly communicated by contrasting the words of a treaty between the United States and the Emperor of China, signed in 1868, with legislation adopted just 14 years later. The Burlingame-Seward Treaty, article V, read: "The United States of America and the Emperor of China cordially recognise the inherent and inalienable right of man to change his home and allegiance, and also the mutual advantage of the free migration and emigration of their citizens and subjects respectively from one country to the other".

Yet, in 1882 Congress passed the Chinese Exclusion Act, one of the most extreme measures ever enacted to stem immigration and one of the first in a long series of U.S. laws designed to determine which groups could enter. Until the late 1800s, immigration to the United States was largely unregulated. In 1875 the Supreme Court decided that regulation of immigration was a federal responsibility. Soon thereafter, in a period of economic downturn, exclusionary measures were passed, including the Chinese Exclusion Act and a law barring people likely to become "public charges." However, despite these regulations, other immigration continued.

In 1924 Congress passed a major immigration act that established the national origins quota system. This law strongly favored Western Europe and all but guaranteed that most legal immigration would be from Europe for the following 40 years. In other actions in early 20th century, the Chinese Exclusion Act was expanded to include the Japanese in 1907 and then most Asian countries, virtually ending immigration from Asia, preventing Asian immigrants from becoming naturalised citizens, and denying them the opportunity to reunite their families. Racism has also played a role in other immigration-related policies and actions.

In the 1930s and 1950s, fears about the "menace" of Mexican immigration led to deportation of almost 4.5 million people of Mexican descent, many of whom were

U.S. citizens or legal residents. Just before World War II, anti- Semitism led to the exclusion of many Jewish refugees who were fleeing Nazi persecution. And during the war, people of Japanese descent, including immigrants and American citizens, were classified as enemy aliens and interned in detention camps.

In 1965 the Immigration and Nationality Act Amendments provided a sweeping change in immigration law. The national origins system was abolished and a new set of priorities for admitting immigrants was adopted. Priority was given to family members of U.S. citizens and permanent residents and to those with skills needed by the U.S. labor market. Race and country of origin were removed as criteria for admission. This important law provided the foundation for the more recent waves of immigration from Asia and Latin America.

Laws passed in the 1980s and 1990s reflect concern with the economic impact of immigration. Seeking to stem illegal migration, the Immigration Reform and Control Act of 1986 introduced employer sanctions for hiring undocumented individuals. However, it also provided for legalisation of several million undocumented immigrants. Again reflecting the ambivalence toward immigration, the Immigration Act of 1990 allowed an increase in the total number of immigrants by adopting a flexible cap of 675,000 per year.

Refugee Admissions

Following the Vietnam War, the United States resettled large numbers of refugees from Vietnam, Laos, and Cambodia, contributing to the significant increase in the U.S. Asian population, both through resettlement and later family reunifications. Significant numbers of refugees also were accepted from Cuba and from the Soviet Union, especially Jewish émigrés who were oppressed by the Soviet government. Refugee policy reflects both important humanitarian efforts and foreign policy priorities. This has been particularly played out in the contrast between treatment of Cubans and Haitians; whereas the former have been welcomed as refugees, Haitians have been interdicted at sea and quickly returned to Haiti. "Haitians who reach the United States without being interdicted are put into fast-track removal procedures, during which they are subject to mandatory detention and are not eligible for release on bond. This package of measures is applied only to Haitians". Haitians are labeled "economic refugees" and therefore are not official refugees under American law, although Haitians may often be in more danger than Cubans who flee.

Three laws passed in 1996 changed the standing of immigrants in U.S. law. Responding to largely unfounded concerns that immigrants were overusing public benefits, the Personal Responsibility and Work Opportunity Reconciliation Act of 1996 "tied the receipt of benefits more directly to citizenship", cutting eligibility for a range of benefits such as food stamps, Medicaid, and supplemental security income. In doing so, the law recast the traditional distinction between legal and illegal immigrants to a new and stark distinction between citizens and legal immigrants. The Illegal Immigration Reform and Immigrant Responsibility Act of 1996 and the Antiterrorism and Effective Death Penalty Act of 1996 contained deportation provisions that have had devastating effects nationally and internationally at both family and societal levels. These laws redefined deportable offenses and retroactively reclassified minor offenses as felonies; deportable offenses include convictions for domestic violence, child abuse, and child neglect.

The laws also removed the right to judicial review in many deportation cases and authorised "expedited removal" of people who arrive at U.S. airports and other borders without proper documents. The impact on families can be devastating; marital partners have been separated, and parents have been deported, leaving their U.S. citizen children without support or parental supervision. The impact of increased deportations has been felt internationally, as countries of origin have been forced to accept deportees with few ties to home and no prospects for jobs or income; in other cases, criminals convicted of serious drug and violent offenses were sent home without warning to officials, unleashing waves of crime.

Again, however, the humanitarianism voice was heard and revisions were underway to soften the loss of entitlements and reconsider judicial review. These were cut short by the terrorist attacks on New York and the Pentagon on September 11, 2001. Fear of terrorism had at least a temporary chilling effect on immigration reform. Liberalisation proposals were abandoned, and sympathy for deportees dried up. The quick adoption of the Uniting and Strengthening America by Providing Appropriate Tools Required to Intercept and Obstruct Terrorism Act of 2001and the issue of executive orders allowed the government to "impose guilt by association on immigrants; authorise the indefinite lock up of aliens on mere suspicion . . . and the use of secret evidence in immigration proceedings that aliens cannot confront or rebut".

Thus, "immigrants from all levels of the social stratum, who share the pain of Americans, have been further victimised by attitudes of intolerance, stereotyping, ethnic profiling and stricter immigration policies". Young Muslim men and those who appeared to be of Middle Eastern heritage were particularly targeted.

The response to concerns about terror included reorganisation of the Immigration and Naturalisation Service, renamed the Bureau of Citizenship and Immigration Services (BCIS); it was moved from the Department of Justice to the newly created Department of Homeland Security. The war on terrorism also has had a major impact on refugee resettlement throughout the world. "In the fallout from the September 2001 attacks in the United States and the subsequent global war on terror, the resettlement program was particularly hard hit . . . Globally, the number of persons resettled under the United Nations High Commission for Refugees (UNHCR) auspices plunged by 56 percent from the previous year". Additional restrictions and long delays have cut the number of international students admitted to the United States.

Challenges of Immigraion Policy

"Migration is an important, complex and multidimensional issue". The challenges of immigration policy are reflected even in international human rights law. The Universal Declaration of Human Rights and subsequent treaties recognise the right to leave one's country as a basic human right. "Everyone has the right to leave any country, including his own, and to return to his country". However, there is no corresponding principle of a right to enter. In his book on immigration, Isbister referred to immigration policy as "inherently immoral."

By that he meant that immigration policies require choices between competing goods or competing evils and often involve the protection of privilege. Deciding whether priority should be given to refugees fleeing oppression or reuniting a longseparated immigrant family or whether amnesty should be granted to the undocumented rather than increasing entry for those who obey the laws are moral and ethical policy dilemmas.

Social workers see the impact of immigrant and refugee policies in their everyday practice. Their very capacity to help and do "good social work" is constrained by immigration policies, especially policies that limit family visitation and family reunification. Deportation policies intervene in social work practice when family offenses become grounds for deportation and thereby impede willingness to report.

Although security concerns have led to excessively restrictive procedures, NASW acknowledges the importance of security and ensuring that those who intend to conduct violent acts are barred from entering the United States. The challenge is to determine the reasonable balance between security and human rights. The United Nations Declaration on the Human Rights of Individuals Who Are Not Nationals of the Country in which They Live, adopted in 1985, specifically states that aliens shall enjoy "the right to life and security of person; no alien shall be subjected to arbitrary arrest or detention".

Procedures to protect security should be within the guidelines of basic human rights protections. Throughout U.S. history, conflicting views about the economic effects of immigration have shaped immigration policies. One view defines immigrants as a drain on the economy and users of public benefits who take needed jobs away from Americans; the opposing view sees immigrants as enhancing the economy through the payment of taxes, investment in small business, and reinvigoration of the rapidly aging U.S. native population. Although most studies show a positive economic effect and some credit relatively high immigration with strengthening the U.S. economic position vis-à-vis Western Europe and Japan,

Isbister cautioned that high rates of immigration may harm low income Americans.

Current debates over possible guest worker programs or provisions to legalise segments of the undocumented population raise additional policy questions. Policies must be developed that provide some relief to long-term resident undocumented families, yet address the fairness implications of providing amnesty to the undocumented that may disadvantage those who "played by the rules." Special care must be taken in the design of guest worker programs not to tie immigrants to potentially abusive and exploitive employers. Refugee policies also need re-examination in the context of 21st century realities. The very definition of *refugee* as one with a "wellfounded fear of persecution on the basis of race, religion, nationality, membership in a particular social group or political opinion" should be reconsidered. If the goal is to protect life, then others, especially those caught up by armed conflict, may have a more compelling need for protection. Historically, U.S. policy has favored involvement in conflicts in Europe over those in Africa and other developing parts of the world. And, the extent to which even the current definition is selectively applied depending on foreign policy considerations should be measured against tests of fairness and equity.

7

School Social Work Methods

Professional Practice

Professional practice relates to the ethical principles, provision of services, and responsibilities that school social workers are expected to maintain.

Standard 1

The school social worker shall demonstrate a recognition of basic human rights, including the right of students to human services; a willingness to act on professional judgment and convictions, and the recognition that change is constant and requires school social workers to remain current by continuously scrutinising and improving theory, policy, and practice.

As integral staff of local education agencies, school social workers have a responsibility to know and comply with local, state, and federal legislation, regulations, and policies.

Standard 2

School social workers shall organise their time, energies, and workloads to fulfill their responsibilities and complete assignments of their position, with due consideration of the priorities among their various responsibilities.

School social workers must manage their work in an efficient and effective manner. Priorities for practice must be developed collaboratively between the school social worker and his or her supervisor. Priorities should be established on the basis of their effect on student needs, the professional skills of the school social worker, program needs, and the availability of other resources. School social workers shall make use of technology systems in the local education agency to enhance communication, obtain and organise information, and demonstrate accountability.

Standard 3

School social workers shall provide consultation to local education agency personnel, school board members, and community representatives to promote understanding and effective utilisation of school social work services.

School social workers provide consultation to facilitate an understanding of factors in the home, local education agency, and community that affect students' educational experiences. They also serve as consultants on such issues as discipline, attendance, confidentiality, race, ethnicity and language, mental health, behavior management, crisis intervention, and child abuse and neglect. School social workers shall constantly be aware of the overall goals, objectives, and tasks of their specialty area and interpret them to local education agency personnel, so that the primary professional activities and competencies of school social workers are maintained.

Standard 4

School social workers shall ensure that students and their families are provided services within the context of multicultural understanding and competence that enhance families' support of students' learning experiences.

Increasing diversity in U.S. classrooms requires that school social workers increase their awareness and appreciation of cultural differences. School social workers must develop competencies that include heightened self-awareness, knowledge, and practice skills.

Standard 5

School social work services shall be extended to students in ways that build students' individual strengths and offer students maximum opportunity to participate in the planning and direction of their own learning experience.

In developing a plan of action, school social workers must consider the characteristics of an individual student and the capacity of all students to communicate about themselves, to choose among options, and to be involved in directing their own learning.

Standard 6

School social workers shall help empower students and their families to gain access to and effectively use formal and informal community resources.

Empowerment is based on the principle of using student and family strengths and structure to enable families to function as advocates for themselves. It is particularly appropriate for school social workers to identify and collaborate with individuals who function as formal or informal leaders in their communities to develop and enhance the natural helping networks that can complement the formal services of the local education agency and community agencies.

Standard 7

School social workers shall maintain adequate safeguards for the privacy and confidentiality of information.

School social workers must be familiar and comply with the various local, state, and federal mandates related to confidentiality. Professional judgment in the use of confidential information shall be based on best practice, legal, and ethical considerations. Students, families, and other professionals should be informed of the confidentiality limitations and requirements when services are initiated.

Standard 8

School social workers shall advocate for students and their families in a variety of situations.

Issues of concern affecting students may include limited educational opportunities; discipline; punitive, arbitrary, and exclusionary policies and procedures in schools; institutional racism; discrimination against and among students based on protected classifications such as race, sex, national origin, sexual orientation, and religion; homophobia; and sexism. Advocacy should support the needs of students who are immigrants and refugees, students who are homeless, students living with HIV/AIDS, students with substance abuse problems, and other at-risk student populations. Effective advocacy can best be accomplished when school social workers are informed about court decisions, legislation, rules and regulations, and policies and procedures that affect school social work practice.

Standard 9

As leaders and members of interdisciplinary teams and coalitions, school social workers shall work collaboratively to mobilise the resources of local education agencies and communities to meet the needs of students and families.

As team leaders and members, school social workers initiate and support activities to overcome institutional barriers and gaps in services. School social workers must demonstrate trust, open communication, mutual respect, ongoing collaboration, and effective coordination to facilitate the achievement of the interdisciplinary team objectives. The unique contribution of the school social worker to the interdisciplinary team is to bring home, school, and community perspectives to the interdisciplinary process.

Standard 10

School social workers shall develop and provide training and educational programs that address the goals and mission of the educational institution.

School social workers shall provide training programs for parents, teachers, other local education agency personnel, and the staff of community agencies. These programs may involve teamwork and collaboration with other disciplines. Content should address the prevention, intervention, and remediation factors that affect students' success in school. School social workers shall support the academic standards of their school districts. This is accomplished through services to prepare students for learning and the actual teaching of social and behavioral skills.

Standard 11

School social workers shall maintain accurate data that are relevant to planning, management, and evaluation of school social work services.

Timely and accurate records document school social work services, demonstrate outcomes, and promote accountability to the local education agency and community. Analyses of activity reports, program statistics, and outcome measures can support the effective use of school social work services to better meet the needs of students and families.

Standard 12

School social workers shall conduct assessments of student needs that are individualised and provide information that is directly useful for designing interventions that address behaviors of concern.

Assessments should take an ecological perspective, focusing on the students, as well as their interactions in the school environment, at home, and in community settings. A functional approach to assessment enhances understanding of the purpose and effect of problematic behaviors and provides information for developing interventions.

Standard 13

School social workers shall incorporate assessments in developing and implementing intervention and evaluation plans that enhance students' abilities to benefit from educational experiences.

Plans are based on assessments relevant to the concerns in the referral and include goals, objectives, and interventions to achieve desired outcomes; methods of evaluation; and outcome criteria. Plans are designed to enhance positive educational experiences and involve the student, the family, other team members, and school and community resources as appropriate.

Standard 14

School social workers, as systems change agents, shall identify areas of need that are not being addressed by the local education agency and community and shall work to create services that address these needs.

School social workers shall initiate activities to address deficiencies in resources and services of the local education agency or community that affect the ability of students to benefit from the educational system.

Advocacy should include leadership on committees and advisory boards at the local, state, and national levels.

Standard 15

School social workers shall be trained in and use mediation and conflict-resolution strategies to promote students' resolution of their nonproductive encounters in the school and community and to promote productive relationships.

Attempts are often made to resolve conflicts and impasses between parents and the local education agency through formal, costly, and often adversarial due process procedures. Mediation and conflict resolution are effective strategies that school social workers should use both to undo the results of nonproductive encounters among students, parents, and school and agency personnel and to build positive, collaborative relationships. School social workers are, by training and experience, well suited to these roles and should seek opportunities to engage in these processes.

Standards for Professional Preparation and Development

Professional preparation defines the level of training required for school social work practice. Professional development refers to the enhancement of basic knowledge and skills that requires ongoing effort by school social workers.

Standard 16

School social workers shall have a graduate degree in social work from a program accredited by the Council on Social Work Education (CSWE). As a distinct specialty within the social work profession, school social work requires specialised knowledge and understanding of educational systems. The school social worker should actively seek this specialised training when the CSWE accredited program does not provide it.

Standard 17

School social workers shall possess knowledge and understanding basic to the social work profession. School social workers shall have an understanding of human behavior in the social environment and be skilled in implementing various practice modalities to help empower disadvantaged and oppressed populations. School social workers shall use research to inform practice and understand social policies related to services in schools.

Standard 18

School social workers shall understand the backgrounds and broad range of experiences that shape students' approaches to learning.

School social workers shall be knowledgeable about child development and biological factors that affect students' ability to function effectively in school. School social workers shall understand the influence of socioeconomic status, gender, culture, disability, and sexual orientation on educational opportunities for students. School social workers also shall understand how emphasizing students' strengths and protective factors can enhance educational success.

Standard 19

School social workers shall possess knowledge and understanding of the organisation and structure of the local education agency.

School social workers shall understand the historical and current perspectives of public school education at the local, state, and national levels, including educational reform and legislation affecting educational opportunity, problems, and policy issues. In addition, school social workers shall be knowledgeable about the financial base of the local education agency, the nature and scope of its authority, and the politics of schoolcommunity relations. School social workers also shall be knowledgeable about approaches to teaching and learning, including standards-based curricula, and the roles and areas of competence of various professionals in the local education agency.

Standard 20

School social workers shall possess knowledge and understanding of the reciprocal influences of home, school, and community.

School social workers shall be knowledgeable about how family dynamics, health, wellness, and mental health; and social welfare policies, programs, and resources in the community affect students' success in the school environment.

Standard 21

School social workers shall possess skills in systematic assessment and investigation. School social workers shall gather data using multiple methods and sources to assess the needs, characteristics, and interactions of students, families, local education agency personnel, individuals, and groups in the neighborhood and community. When appropriate, school social workers shall collect information to document and assess aspects of the biological, medical, psychological, cultural, sociological, emotional, legal, and environmental factors that affect students' learning. School social workers shall integrate biopsychosocial assessment data into reports that include educationally relevant recommendations as well as performance objectives and measurable outcomes as needed.

Standard 22

School social workers shall understand the relationship between practice and policies affecting students.

School social workers shall be knowledgeable about current and proposed policies, analyse their effect on students, and advocate for policies that maximise student success.

Standard 23

School social workers shall be able to select and apply empirically validated or promising prevention and intervention methods to enhance students' educational experiences.

School social workers shall possess skills to assess problems and determine whether interventions should occur at the primary, secondary, or tertiary level. School social work practice should be based on empirically supported interventions.

Standard 24

School social workers shall be able to evaluate their practice and disseminate the findings to consumers, the local education agency, the community, and the profession.

Using scholarly literature or program research designs, school social workers shall evaluate interventions and share findings with consumers, local education agency administrators, the community, and other school social workers through in-service training, conferences, and professional publications.

Standard 25

School social workers shall possess skills in developing coalitions at the local, state, and national levels that promote student success.

School social workers shall be able to work with individuals, groups, and organisations that have diverse interests, but whose common purpose is to develop programs or systems of care that support and enhance the health, social and emotional well-being, and safety of students.

Standard 26

School social workers shall be able to promote collaboration among community health and mental health services providers and facilitate student access to these services.

School social workers shall support the development and implementation of comprehensive school-based and school-linked programs (for example, full-service schools, full-service community schools, family resource centers, community schools, schoolbased health clinics) that promote student health and mental health. School social workers shall be able to address issues such as information sharing and accountability and shall be able to coordinate community resources that support student success.

Standard 27

School social workers shall assume responsibility for their own continued professional development. To practice effectively, school social workers must remain knowledgeable of reforms in education and best practice models in the social work profession.

Standard 28

School social workers shall contribute to the development of the profession by educating and supervising school social work interns. School social workers may provide field instruction through the supervision of school social work interns and through the provision of other appropriate learning experiences in relation to school social work practice.

Standards for Administrative Structure and Support

An effective school social work program must have adequate administrative structure and support. NASW recommends that the local education agency use the following standards, along with state and federal guidelines, to develop a school social work program.

Standard 29

State departments of education or other state entities that license or certify educational personnel shall regulate school social work practice. To ensure competent provision of school social work services, state departments of education or other state entities that license or certify educational personnel should make sure that the credentials of individuals charged with providing these services adhere to the standards of practice and are reciprocal and uniform.

Standard 30

State departments of education or other state entities that license or certify educational personnel shall employ a state school social work consultant who is a credentialed and experienced school social worker.

State education agencies are responsible for providing local education agencies with leadership and technical assistance to ensure all students an equal opportunity to achieve optimal success in the educational environment. State education agencies should provide a school social work consultant to collaborate with other service programs within the state education agency and other state agencies; influence legislative and regulatory efforts related to education; represent the state in regional, state, and national activities related to school social work; ensure that school social work programs are integrated with other school programs statewide; provide technical assistance to local education agencies in the development and implementation of school social work programs; provide leadership and technical assistance in the development of practice and credentialing standards for school social workers; and advocate for inclusion of school social work programs and services at the local education agency level.

Standard 31

School social work services shall be provided by credentialed school social workers employed by the local education agency. School social work services should be provided by individuals designated as credentialed school social workers and employed by local education agencies. Local education agencies should ensure that school social work services are aligned with educational goals and integrated with other school support services.

Standard 32

Local education agencies shall employ school social workers with the highest level of qualifications for entry-level practitioners.

A master of social work (MSW) degree is the recommended entry-level qualification for school social work. When the local education agency employs school social workers whose highest degree is a bachelor of social work (BSW) in addition to school social workers with the MSW degree, tasks should be assigned differentially. Assignments must take into account levels of education and demonstrated competence and be consistent with the legal regulation of professional social work practice within a given state. Both the MSW degree and the BSW degree should be received from a program accredited by CSWE.

Standard 33

Social workers in schools shall be designated "school social workers."

"School social worker" is the position title that correctly identifies the educational background, profession, and function of a social worker employed by the local education agency. Other titles, such as "attendance officer," "pupil personnel worker," "home and school visitor," "homeschool coordinator," "visiting teacher," "family collaborative worker," "family specialist," or "home-family specialist," project incomplete or misleading notions of the school social worker's qualifications and functions.

Standard 34

Salaries and job classifications of school social workers shall be commensurate with their education, experience, and responsibilities and be comparable to similarly qualified professional personnel employed by the local education agency.

Procedures used in setting school social workers' salaries must be equitable and responsive to the levels of education, experience, and responsibilities of the school social workers.

Standard 35

The administrative structure established by the local

education agency shall provide for appropriate school social work supervision.

The local education agency is responsible for administrative and professional supervision to ensure high-quality services. Supervision of school social work programs should be provided by credentialed and experienced MSW school social workers.

Standard 36

The administrative structure of the local education agency shall delineate clear lines of support and accountability for the school social work program.

The administrative structure and organisation of the local education agency should provide for optimum use of school social work knowledge and skills. Realistic job descriptions, working conditions, and workload standards are essential, as is a mechanism for regular review of goals, objectives, accomplishments, and accountability procedures of the school social work program. Designation of a lead social worker can help promote appropriate support and accountability.

Standard 37

The local education agency shall provide a professional work setting that allows school social workers to practice effectively.

School social workers require basic work resources to ensure privacy and confidentiality for students and families. These basic resources include an office; clerical support; up-to-date information technology; an adequate budget for professional materials, supplies, and activities; and adequate space at each school site for meeting with students, families, and local education agency personnel.

Standard 38

The local education agency shall provide opportunities for school social workers to engage in professional development activities that support school social work practice.

Funding support and an adequate number of professional leave days enable school social workers to strengthen and broaden skills required to better serve students, families, the local education agency, and the community.

Standard 39

The goals, objectives, and tasks of a school social work program shall be clearly and directly related to the mission of the local education agency and the educational process.

School social workers are expected to support and help facilitate educational reforms and initiatives, particularly those that emphasize prevention, early intervention, parent education and involvement, service integration, partnerships, and support for student transitions.

Standard 40

The local education agency shall involve school social workers in developing and coordinating partnerships with community health, mental health, and social services providers linked with or based at school sites to ensure that these services promote student educational success.

Because of their extensive knowledge of community resources, school social workers should play a critical role in facilitating the provision of community services in the local education agency. School social workers help build effective school-community teams at school sites by addressing issues such as roles, responsibilities, and supervision of team members, and by developing procedures to ensure confidentiality, documentation, and accountability. School social workers also help orient community providers to school climate, culture, and structure, and to the laws and regulations governing practice in educational settings.

Standard 41

All programs incorporating school social work services shall require ongoing evaluation to determine their contribution to the educational success of all students.

Through ongoing evaluation, school social workers demonstrate accountability to the students and families they serve, the educational system and community, and the standards and ethics of the social work profession. Methods used to evaluate social work practice should be assessed periodically to ensure that objectives, activities, and measured outcomes are aligned with the local education agency's goals. School social work documentation should be reviewed periodically to ensure accurate recording of functions, tasks, activities, and measured outcomes.

Standard 42

The local education agency shall establish and implement a school social work-student population ratio to ensure reasonable workload expectations.

The local education agency shall provide a level of school social work services that is sufficient to address the nature and extent of student needs. Appropriate ratios for school social work staff to students should depend on the characteristics and needs of the student population to be served. Each local or state education agency should establish adequate levels and types of school social work services on the basis of comprehensive needs assessment data.

Ethical Principles

The following broad ethical principles are based on social work's core values of service, social justice, dignity and worth of the person, importance of human relationships, integrity, and competence. These principles set forth ideals to which all social workers should aspire.

Value: Service

Ethical Principle: **Social workers' primary goal is to help people in need and to address social problems.**

Social workers elevate service to others above self-interest. Social workers draw on their knowledge, values, and skills to help people in need and to address social problems. Social workers are encouraged to volunteer some portion of their professional skills with no expectation of significant financial return.

***Value:* Social Justice**

Ethical Principle: Social workers challenge social injustice.

Social workers pursue social change, particularly with and on behalf of vulnerable and oppressed individuals and groups of people. Social workers' social change efforts are focused primarily on issues of poverty, unemployment, discrimination, and other forms of social injustice. These activities seek to promote sensitivity to and knowledge about oppression and cultural and ethnic diversity. Social workers strive to ensure access to needed information, services, and resources; equality of opportunity; and meaningful participation in decision making for all people.

***Value:* Dignity and Worth of the Person**

***Ethical Principle:* Social workers respect the inherent dignity and worth of the person.**

Social workers treat each person in a caring and respectful fashion, mindful of individual differences and cultural and ethnic diversity. Social workers promote clients' socially responsible self-determination. Social workers seek to enhance clients' capacity and opportunity to change and to address their own needs. Social workers are cognisant of their dual responsibility to clients and to the broader society. They seek to resolve conflicts between clients' interests and the broader society's interests in a socially responsible manner consistent with the values, ethical principles, and ethical standards of the profession.

***Value:* Importance of Human Relationships**

Ethical Principle: Social workers recognise the central importance of human relationships.

Social workers understand that relationships between and among people are an important vehicle for change. Social workers engage people as partners in the helping process. Social workers seek to strengthen relationships among people in a purposeful effort to promote, restore, maintain, and enhance the well-being of individuals, families, social groups, organisations, and communities.

***Value:* Integrity**

Ethical Principle: *Social workers behave in a trustworthy manner.*

Social workers are continually aware of the profession's mission, values, ethical principles, and ethical standards and practice in a manner consistent with them. Social workers act honestly and responsibly and promote ethical practices on the part of the organisations with which they are affiliated.

Value: **Competence**

Ethical Principle: **Social workers practice within their areas of competence and develop and enhance their professional expertise.**

Social workers continually strive to increase their professional knowledge and skills and to apply them in practice. Social workers should aspire to contribute to the knowledge base of the profession.

8

Multiple Social Services Practices

The relationship between people who are chronic offenders and who come into multiple contacts with social service agencies is important for several reasons. First, as the classic study by Wolfgang, Figlio and Sellin demonstrated, the social implications of chronic offending among juveniles are socially dismal both for the offenders and for the wider community. Second, the economic and social costs of chronic offending and multiple service use are high. As an extreme example, Horin reported that the Department of Community Services is paying $800,000 per year for the care and treatment of one especially difficult child, and $400,000 for three others. They may imply a revolving door of less-than-optimal responses by service agencies. Third, the presence of a small number of chronic offenders who are multiple service users may imply they are not receiving responses that would be most effective for them. Fourth, ineffective allocation of resources may deprive other people in need of help from receiving essential services. It is imperative that the most efficient and effective means of treatment are being utilised. The broader need for precious services throughout the society must not be sacrificed. Fifth, the causal relationship between chronic offending and the use of multiple services is unclear. While conventional wisdom could fault the failure of effective services for preventing recidivism, the offending itself may initiate the provision of services. Finally, understanding the relationship between chronic offending and multiple service use is vital to create and maintain programs and to direct policies that will help to:

— identify areas where current research and inquiry are lacking;
— establish mechanisms for collecting and analysing data
— prevent offending, facilitate rehabilitation and reduce recidivism; and
— present a broad and thorough discussion about the relationship between being a chronic offender and being a multiple user of social services.

Two general complementary frameworks have been used to consider how chronic offenders draw upon supportive services. These approaches constitute complementary rather than antagonistic research strategies. The first is an actuarial approach that analyses characteristics that place people at highest risk of offending and encountering social service institutions. The logic of the actuarial analysis implies establishing probabilities of how underlying characteristics predispose people to offend and to come into contact with social services. The actuarial approach is a powerful tool for examining large amounts of information and describing the relationship between offending and service use for an entire population or subpopulations.

Social scientists have scarcely begun to examine the abundant valid and reliable social data that are available in Australia. Actuarial analysis is convenient because it relies on systematically collected government records. One finding that has emerged through the actuarial approach is that chronic offenders are likely to have multiple characteristics that are associated with encountering difficulties in many contexts in addition to the legal system. These factors; age, gender, family dysfunction, ethnic and cultural status and mental illness, are discussed in the following section.

The second framework is a clinical approach that scrutinises the personal histories of offending and service use for individuals. The clinical approach provides valuable insights into individual experiences with justice and other social service institutions that cannot be obtained from the actuarial approach. The advantage of this approach is that by identifying the actual experiences of individuals a case history can be constructed for each individual. There also are disadvantages. The cases may not be representative of other offenders or service users.

The broad perspective about what behaviours characterise the larger population may be diminished because the cases under investigation may not represent what is occurring in the larger population. Ethical problems also plague the disclosure of information about individuals. However, the clinical approach can provide complex and profound insights into individual experiences with justice and other social service institutions that cannot be obtained from the actuarial approach.

Several underlying factors have implications regarding causation and consequent treatments of chronic offending. References are drawn from research that reported initial discoveries of the findings being interpreted and from recent data from Australia. Offenders with these characteristics may be more likely to draw upon services besides the social justice system because of other underlying vulnerabilities. Persistent disruptive effects of chronic offending into adulthood and parenthood are of particular concern. Chronically offending juveniles are more likely to become adults who abuse drug and alcohol, offend, suffer from physical and mental illness, divorce and die younger.

Age

Offending in general and chronic offending in particular are strongly associated with age. Offending peaks in the United States between 15 and 24 and rapidly declines with age. While more sophisticated and professionally skilled offenders, such as forgers and embezzlers, tend to be older, approximately two thirds of robberies, burglaries, arson and vehicle thefts, and about half of all violent crimes, are committed by people under 25. In Queensland, South Australia and Victoria the 2001-2002 alleged offender rate per 100,000 was roughly four times higher for 15-19 year olds than for the total offender rate. In Queensland the peak ages for juvenile male (42%) and female (35%) offenders, respectively, were 16 and 15. Although reductions in offending occurred among the 10-14 (-26%) and 15-19 (-22%) year olds between 1995-92 and 2001-02, chronic offending did not decline.

Considerable disagreement exists about the reasons for this 'inverted *j*' relationship between age and offending. Most authors agree that some combination of motivations to offend and an absence of constraints predispose individual offenders. Young people who offend are especially likely to be in the company of other young offenders 4 who are acting beyond conventional control mechanisms. The consistent relationship found between age (and gender) and crime increases the validity of biological explanations and weakens general social theories. Age also is linked to having accidents, pregnancies, mental illness and school problems, all of which may lead youth to draw upon social services.

Gender

Males are much more likely to commit crimes, to commit

more serious crimes and to do so more frequently than women. The male/female ratio for violent crime (5.7) and total crime (3.1) exemplify this difference. In Queensland, South Australia and Victoria the alleged offender rate per 100,000 was roughly four times higher for males (3033) than for females (753). Lynch, Buckman and Krenske found that female young offenders who entered the Queensland justice system in 1994 (22%) were less than half as likely to be imprisoned in adulthood as males (54%). With few exceptions, including prostitution and shoplifting, the differential between men and women is among the most documented in criminology, though some theorists maintain some convergence is occurring. In Australia declines have occurred among younger offenders of both genders. Men, especially young men, are particularly at higher risk of accidents and problems with school than are women. These risks would increase their likelihood to interact with social services.

Minority Status

Ethnic and racial crime statistics are among the most controversial in criminology for two reasons. First, definitions of minority status are imprecise. Second, criminal justice statistics likely imply labels that operate to the disfavour of some minorities. In the United States Black people are approximately two to four times as likely to commit index crimes as White people. Indigenous People often have comparatively higher rates of crime and reoffending. American and Canadian Indians are more than twice as likely to be imprisoned, and New Zealand Maoris more than three times as likely, as White people. Australian Aborigines and Torres Strait Islanders are twelve times as likely to be incarcerated. In the Queensland study, additional orders were served to seventy-nine per cent (89% for males) of young Indigenous offenders additional orders compared to forty-nine per cent of non-Indigenous offenders. Measures of social disadvantage among Indigenous Peoples correspond to their crime statistics. Their increased probabilities of experiencing problems in school, familial relationships, employment, housing and health are likely to bring them into more frequent contact with representatives in those sectors.

Offenders also differ with regard to ethnicity in Australia.For example, migrants from Turkey, Lebanon, and Vietnam are more likely to commit crimes than those from Greece, Africa and Eire. In 1996-97 migrants from Romania had the highest rate per 1000 (92) of offending in Victoria. In contrast, migrants from the United Kingdom had a relatively low (13) offending rate. Overall, migrants have lower rates of crime than do native-born Australians (31), a figure which includes Indigenous offenders. Information about second-generation migrants would be even more instructive because the consequences of ethnic marginality on crime and social services would become more evident. Migrants are entitled to, and are more likely to draw upon, a variety of social services. Migrants who enter Australia as skilled employees draw on fewer resources than migrants who follow as family members or who are admitted under the humanitarian program. Comparisons of offending and service use among migrants who enter in these different streams would provide valuable information.

Intelligence

Intelligence, as measured by intelligence quotient (IQ), has consistently been found to be negatively associated with criminal behaviour. The linkage is contentious. IQ is affected by cultural and personal experiences in addition to reflecting a middle class bias. Nevertheless, with the exception of crimes that reward levels of intellectual expertise, like white-collar crime and forgery, persons with lower IQ scores are more likely to offend and to be apprehended. Lower intelligence reduces educational success and consequent economic and social success. It also may reduce social awareness and exacerbate the chances of persons with low IQ to be labelled. For these reasons, persons with lower intelligence may need more special service assistance.

Mental Illness, Personality and Temperament

A connection between mental illness and crime, especially violence, has been investigated for decades. The findings, however, are neither strong nor direct. Mental illness implies difficulty in conforming, though only a minority of mentally ill people commit crimes. Impulsivity and psychopathy are associated with criminal behaviour. Research indicates that some criminal behaviour, such as drug use, sexual abuse and violence, alleviate anxiety induced by the illness. Participation in these activities also increases interaction with antisocial peers who impulsively use more drugs, experiment more with sex and perform more poorly in school than other juveniles. In their recent meta-analysis of twins and adopted children, Rhee and Waldman provide strong evidence that while genetics contributes to antisocial behaviour, the influences of environmental factors are much greater.

How mental illness is defined can dramatically influence how it is associated with crime. The New South Wales Inmate Health Study found that most men (78.2%) and women (90.1%) inmates suffered from some psychiatric disorder at the time of reception. Mullen (2001) found that these disorders were compounded by extremely high levels of drug and alcohol abuse compounded these disorders. In contrast, less than one

Australian homicide in twenty (4.4 %) was found to be committed by a person suffering from a mental disorder.

Drugs

Although experimentation with drugs is common among youth, heavy and persistent use typifies criminal offenders. The Drug Use Careers of Offenders (DUCO) study in Australia found that most male offenders were multiple offenders who had used drugs (62%) during the six months before being apprehended. As found in prior studies, the most chronic offenders in the DUCO study began using drugs and offending at earlier ages than other offenders.

Family and Community Dysfunction

The Gluecks' had also noted negative effects of dysfunctional families on reoffending, though disagreement about what constitutes functional persists. Children in single-parent households are ten to fifteen percent more likely to be delinquents than children from intact families, though children of divorced parents are less likely to be delinquent than those from unhappily intact families. Broken homes are less likely to provide adequate supervision and effective socialisation than intact homes. Poor families have more frequently been disrupted by divorce and loss of family members and health problems. Single mothers and their families are more likely to experience social and psychological disruption from unemployment, as well as unsettling changes in residence, employment and household composition. Dysfunctional may also imply parents who are socially and emotionally neglectful and parents who use drugs. Chronic offenders are significantly more likely to come from deviant and multiple problem families.

THEORETICAL ISSUES

Motivations and controls to conform are influenced by social factors, such as the type of community, family and peer interactions, and individual factors, such as personality, intelligence and mental health. Factors that increase the frequency of offending also increase the frequency of chronic offending. As the number of underlying factors characterising a person increase, so too does their likelihood to offend. Just as being an older mentally healthy woman living in a supportive and nurturing environment decreases the likelihood of being a chronic offender, being a young, mentally unstable, male addict residing in a highly disorganised neighbourhood increases the likelihood.

Most sociological and psychological research has indicated that chronic offending usually is a consequence of ineffective controls and socialisation. An alternative perspective claims that chronic offenders represent a failure of government. Ogilvie distinguished *governmentalised* youth, who are identified through their involvement with the service system, from those who are identified as *marginalised* because they are homeless. Noting their frequent progression from family related services to trouble with the legal system, she suggested that social services for youth might be made more effective. White observed that the frequency and basis with which young people interact with police services, housing services, welfare agencies and other social services affects their health and wellbeing. Young people who have been state wards frequently become enmeshed in the juvenile justice system.

White posited two general pathways to chronic offending. Some young people offend as a reaction against their *negative experiences* with social justice services. Others offend because they have been *deprived of resources* that could have helped them. Most chronic offenders come from backgrounds that impede softer sentencing options. Their homes are often so dysfunctional that they are placed into foster care for lack of more nurturing alternatives. A cycle of multiple foster care placements, school and adjustment problems and eventually multiple offending occurs because of their unstable families and unsupportive communities. The key research questions from this alternative perspective involve how the experiences of young multiple service users impact upon their material circumstances and how these experiences influence their disposition toward (or away from) criminal and anti-social behaviour.

Motivations and controls to conform are influenced by social factors, such as the type of community, family and peer interactions that affect a person, and individual factors, such as personality, intelligence and mental health. However, the flaw in adapting an overly sociological interpretation of risk is that many persons who are in high risk categories are not multiple offenders, whether they are receiving multiple services or not.

Initiatives for Reducing Chronic Offending and Multiple Service Use

Criminology faces a quandary regarding how to respond to offenders, particularly chronic offenders who draw heavily upon social services. 'Nothing works' became the pessimistic conservative invective regarding rehabilitation throughout the 1980's in American criminology. Gendreau, Little & Goggin demonstrated through meta-analysis the more humane position that rehabilitation initiatives can reduce recidivism. Nevertheless, this more optimistic position was subverted in the United States and to some extent in Australia.

The recognition that some offenders have especially high potential for reoffending is important. Carcach and Leverett found that recidivism declined when service orders were imposed. Government policy has placed some mentally ill people at greater risk of offending. The positive side of deinstitutionalisation has been that far fewer people are institutionalised. Between 1981 and 2001 the number of people in psychiatric hospitals or other mental institutions dropped from 20,170 to 6,100. However, deinstitutionalisation may have eventuated in offending and consequent incarceration of mentally ill persons who in the past would have been institutionalised. Victoria has recently written an act establishing a model for service delivery among chronically offending adults who are multiple service users. A juvenile treatment model in New Zealand is currently being trialed.

Costs of Offending and the Provision of Services

If estimating the magnitude of the relationship between chronic offending and multiple service use is difficult, attempting to estimate the costs of the relationship multiplies that difficulty. Several factors contribute to this increased difficulty. The costs of crime and of the provision of services are themselves difficult to estimate. The meanings of costs and benefits further complicate those estimates. The following discussion projects how general estimates are associated with more specific costs for chronic offenders who are multiple offenders.

The most definitive current estimate is that crime costs Australia approximately $32 billion per year. Mayhew's estimate is conservative since many expensive crimes were not included in the calculations. In addition to direct costs of items destroyed and lost, costs resulting from medical treatment, loss of work and policing, court and confinement and less tangible costs add to the figure.

The estimated costs vary according to type of offence. For example, homicide costs approximately $1.6 million per offence, assaults about $1,800, robbery about $3,600 and vehicle theft about $6,000. Crimes vary also in the proportion that they contribute to overall costs. For example, fraud contributes 31 per cent of the total, violence 14 per cent, drug misuse 10 per cent and robbery 3 per cent. General estimates are imprecise and subject to wider variation. The United Nations estimates the cost of a homicide in Australia to be US$ 829,000 in comparison to Mayhew's higher estimate. The costs of incarceration are a major contributor to the costs of crime and are much easier to estimate. The cost per prisoner per day ranged from $108.40 in Queensland to $195.9 in the ACT, and averaged $139.50 for Australia in 2001. Two counter trends are evident. At the same time that alternatives are diverting more offenders from incarceration, the number of persons imprisoned has increased by nearly one-third because of increased numbers of offences and offenders.

In addition to costs of crime, this makes it necessary to address the costs of service delivery among chronic offenders who draw heavily upon social services. The rather benign act of leaving school early costs the Australian economy $2 billion a year. The costs of the ubiquitous abuse of drugs was $1.9 billion over a decade ago, and that cost had increased by more than a quarter during the previous four years. The individual and collective social costs are very high. Approximately one death in five is drug related. Weatherburn et al estimate that a heroin user who ingests three caps per day must raise between $30 and $40 thousand per year.

Nevertheless, however the costs are defined and whatever the measures employed, the costs are high. The unresolved empirical problem involves discovering what proportion of costs and what kinds of costs are associated with chronic offenders who frequently draw upon other social services. It also requires determining the characteristics of those social services.

The economic and social costs of chronic offending and multiple service use may imply a revolving door of costly and less-than-optimal responses by service agencies. As an extreme example, Horin reported that the Department of Community Services is paying $800,000 per year for the care and treatment of one especially difficult child, and $400,000 for three others. Identification of costs for particular groups of offenders and service users who are participating in rehabilitation initiatives may lead to reductions in costs associated with receiving special treatment. More importantly, they may lead to lower recidivism rates, which would reduce direct costs of crime, indirect costs of treatment and rehabilitation, and secondary costs to victims. For example, the individual cost ($143.87 per day) of participating in the NSW Drug Court Program in 2000 was only marginally less than the cost of conventional sanctions ($151.72). However, the longer-term savings from reduced recidivism make the program much more cost effective.

If such offenders are more likely to engage in particular types of crime, they may be proportionately more (or less) costly to society, depending on the costs of such crimes. If they are more likely to require special types of incarceration, such as forensics care or top-security, the costs may be three or four times as costly. On the other hand, if forensic care significantly reduces recidivism, the additional expenditures may be justified in beneficial economic, as well as humanistic, terms. Similarly, certain types of crime prevention may be particularly applicable and effective for chronic offenders with multiple service needs. For each aspect of responding to different types of crime and with different aspects of prevention and corrections, the differential costs of chronic offenders and multiple service users can be analysed. Based on what is known about the social and demographic characteristics of offenders, it is likely that most chronic offenders who are multiple service users may be relatively more likely to commit a disproportionate number of relatively low cost crimes while drawing upon a relatively high proportion of expensive social and justice services. For example, the direct economic costs of crimes committed by juveniles are relatively low in comparison to total crime, which is rare among juveniles. However, the justice and service costs for juveniles are collectively high in comparison to overall costs of, for example, fraud.

9

Social Work Strategies for Child and Family Welfare

Social work with children and families is defined here as activity undertaken by a professionally qualified social worker. It does not include other activities undertaken by or on behalf of a social work department. Work with children and families must be set within the broader framework of social work as a whole. This blends together knowledge from a range of disciplines: social administration, sociology, psychology, human development, ethics and law. Its practitioners develop working knowledge of systems, organisations and national and local resources. They learn skills in building relationships, communication, advocacy, organisation and administration. Importantly, underpinning values require its practitioners to develop empathy and respect for people as unique individuals. The British Association of Social Workers' Code of Ethics for Social Work's value on human dignity and worth states:

> Every human being has intrinsic value. All persons have a right to well-being, to self-fulfilment and to as much control over their own lives as is consistent with the rights of others.

None of these items is unique to social work but the blend offers a particular approach to people in difficulty.

Practice experience shows us that, at its best, this approach enables obstacles to be overcome and positive outcomes to be achieved. Social work with children and families is about the whole child in the family, taking account of all the surrounding circumstances.

Desired or desirable outcomes for children are taken as the starting point. For the state the prime focus for work with children and families is the well-being of the children. The Children (Scotland) Act 1995 sets out in section 1(1), '...a parent has in relation to his child the responsibility (a) to safeguard and promote the child's health, development and welfare...' and in section 20(1) (a) requires that local authorities 'promote and safeguard the welfare of children in need in their area (b) so far as consistent with that duty promote the upbringing of children by their families'. More recently, the Commissioner for Children and Young People (Scotland) Act 2003 section 5(3) indicates that 'The Commissioner must, in particular, (a) regard, and encourage others to regard, the best interests of children and young people as a primary consideration'. The crucial contribution of parents' well-being becomes apparent as the discussion proceeds.

'For Scotland's Children' indicates that by the end of the journey to adulthood each child should have reached his/her potential in terms of emotional and social maturity, be in good health, and have attained a level of academic achievement and other skills. The Scottish Executive's guidance for integrated children's services plans sets out seven areas of aspiration for Scotland's children and young people:

— *Safe:* Children and young people should be protected from abuse, neglect and harm by others at home, at school and in the community.
— *Nurtured:* Children and young people should live within a supportive family setting, with additional

assistance if required, or where this is not possible, within another caring setting, ensuring a positive and rewarding child hood experience.

- *Healthy:* Children and young people should enjoy the highest attainable standards of physical and mental health, with access to suitable healthcare and support for safe and healthy lifestyle choices.
- *Achieving:* Children and young people should have access to positive learning environments and opportunities to develop their skills, confidence and self esteem to the fullest potential.
- *Active:* Children and young people should be active with opportunities and encouragement to participate in play and recreation, including sport.
- *Respected and responsible:* Children, young people and their carers should be involved in decisions that affect them, should have their voices heard and should be encouraged to play an active and responsible role in their communities.
- *Included:* Children, young people and their carers should have access to high quality services, when required, and should be assisted to overcome the social, educational, physical, environmental and economic barriers that create inequality.

Similarly, the Westminster government's policy, Every Child Matters, sets out five priority outcomes for children and young people:

- *being healthy:* enjoying good physical and mental health and living a healthy lifestyle;
- *staying safe:* being protected from harm and neglect; having security and stability and being cared for;
- *enjoying and achieving:* getting the most out of life and developing skills for adulthood; enjoying school

and recreation; achieving national education standards;

- *making a positive contribution:* being involved with the community and society and not engaging in antisocial or offending behaviour; developing positive relationships; developing self-confidence and dealing with life changes and challenges;
- *economic well-being:* not being prevented by economic disadvantage from achieving their full potential in life; access to transport and material goods; living in households free from low income.

These choices of .outcome reflect to some extent the United Nations Convention on the Rights of the Child. In particular, it is possible immediately to identify the right to be protected from abuse and neglect, the right to the highest level of health possible and to health and medical services, the right to an adequate standard of living, the right to education and the right to leisure, play and participation in cultural and artistic activities.

Further, in its Looking After Children materials and Framework for the Assessment of Children in Need and their Families, the Department of Health set out seven dimensions of development crucial to children's well-being: health, education, emotional and behavioural development, identity, family and social relationships, social presentation and self care skills. These were developed in response to an expanding body of research about what is important for children and concern about how little was really known about the impact of public care on children. The materials were piloted with parents and professionals and there was assent to the validity of the dimensions.

Obstacles may be found at the level of the individual child, the parent(s), family, wider family, community or on account of broader social conditions. A genetic condition or disability caused by disease or accident may prevent a child reaching desired outcomes. The physical or mental ill health of a parent, substance abuse by a parent, the absence of a parent or disharmony in the parents' relationship may impinge on the outcomes for a particular child, as may serious illness or a death in the wider family. Lack of support from wider family and/or friends, living in a community characterised by poverty, crime or anti social behaviour may also have a negative affect on the outcomes for children. Racism or general antipathy to the poor in a society that measures value by economic wealth may further disadvantage children who fall outside the preferred group.

A child may be affected by any number of these, and other similar, conditions simultaneously or at different times in childhood. The interplay between the child's developmental needs, parenting capacity and the environment are recognised in the Framework for Assessing Children in Need and their Families as affecting outcomes. These needs may present in a number of ways. Writing about the matching needs and services method of planning for children in need, Jo Tunnard helpfully identifies in order of their relative size, 'a fairly typical set of need groups from a local authority audit of children newly referred to social services'. The need groups are:

- for practical support;
- for help to parents to gain confidence in parenting;
- for help with resolving adult conflict;
- for help to ensure children receive better care;
- for help to resolve tension between parents and children;
- for help to deal with emotional problems and mental health issues;

- for support because of a child or parent's illness or disability;
- for help to improve or control a child's behaviour;
- for help to deal with loss or trauma;
- for immediate protection of the child;
- to help parents or older children to stop or reduce a substance misuse; and
- to assist asylum seekers.

Alternatively, the Scottish Executive's Guidance for Integrated Children's Services Plans sets out a list of examples of children in need, including some that would fall into Hardiker's level four need, for example children looked after. Others might fall into levels two and three depending on the how far an individual situation had deteriorated e.g. children/young people in poor housing, children who have emotional and mental health problems. In most cases the need descriptions themselves include obstacles to good outcomes e.g. children affected by the imprisonment of a family member, young runaways, and it is notable, though to be expected, that very few of the needs listed would be met simply by universal services.

Need for Social Work Intervention

There are threefold categorisation of the need for social work applies to children and families. The need arises when parents:

1. know they face obstacles to achieving the outcomes they want for their children's development or to keeping them safe, but:
   - they, their families, their support networks or communities cannot overcome them

- the costs (physical, emotional, social and financial) to them are too high in the short, medium or longer term
- the resources needed are so specialised that they are only available through social work or medical assessment;

2. do not recognise that there are ways of overcoming the obstacles to their children's development or safety either partially or completely; and
3. seek, or their behaviour creates, outcomes for their children that are contrary to legislation and regulation.

As children grow older and begin to have more responsibility for their own wellbeing it may be they, as well as or instead of their parents, who fall into the categories outlined. In all three situations it is most likely that social work will need to be provided to both children and parents.

Aspects of Social Work Intervention

There are different stages and aspects of social work intervention with children and families.

Identifying the problem to be overcome

The first stage to overcoming obstacles is to recognise and describe the problem and acknowledge that change is needed. Social workers can assist the family to identify the issues using empathy and problem solving skills. In any of the situations outlined in 2.4 there may be a number of factors impinging on the parents' or child's capacity to overcome obstacles and achieve desired outcomes. Some may be immediately apparent. Others may be more difficult to discern. It is likely that neither parent nor child is aware of all the elements contributing to difficulties. They may be oblivious to the consequences that may ensue if difficulties remain unresolved. Particularly in cases referred by others for local authority social work intervention, the family may desire outcomes that conflict with legislation and/or social work's responsibilities to protect or control.

For example, children or parents may be using prohibited substances, parents views of child care may leave children wandering the streets at an age and/or times which put them at risk. Social work's distinctive contribution here is to use empathy, communication and relationship skills to achieve acknowledgement that change is needed. A change in organisational response may be required. Both individuals and organisations may need to be convinced of the need for change.

Assessing the situation

At an early stage of contact social work involves assessment of the child and family's situation through appraisal of what is seen and heard in contact with the family in and out of the home, through careful interviewing, enabling members of the family to express their feelings and views, and through communication with other organisations and professionals in contact with the family. The social worker will lead the family through the process, highlighting and explaining the importance of examining the various kinds of information.

Social workers will use a range of knowledge, models and frameworks to decide what information is needed and to assess the information collected. To ensure that necessary information is collected social workers need to establish working relationships of trust with family and professionals. They must be able to understand the cultures and attitudes of all those they involve, through their own knowledge and skill, or by drawing on that of others.

Assessment continues throughout contact and involvement with children and families. Recognition and understanding of behavioural patterns, systems of communication and patterns of events over time are vital to successful outcomes. In situations referred to the local authority for intervention the social worker may have difficulty in engaging the family's cooperation and interest. Social work skills and persistence are needed to find the key to engagement.

In recognition of the difficulties inherent in achieving effective assessments the Department of Health introduced the Framework for the Assessment of Children in Need and their Families.

Macdonald notes the pitfalls that arise when conducting assessments. It is not enough simply to follow a framework setting out the areas to be investigated, social workers need to exercise professional judgement and be alert to unconscious bias which may creep into the work, distorting assessments and the degree of risk.

The Department for Education and Skills is developing a Common Assessment Framework to help ensure that all children achieve the outcomes set out in Every Child Matters:

> 'Through the CAF, we intend to implement a common approach to needs assessment that can be used by the whole children's workforce, whether they are in universal or specialist services, for any child in need of support. Its aim will be to provide a mechanism whereby any practitioner working with a child or young person can conduct a good quality, but relatively non-specialised, assessment of unmet needs and, where appropriate, share it with other agencies. It aims to provide a non-bureaucratic 'whole child' assessment...
>
> 'Common assessment would also essentially form a front-end to more specialist assessments, which would themselves need modification to accommodate the standards imposed by the CAF.'

It is recognised that the CAF will need to have a relationship to responsibilities to promote and safeguard the well-being of children in need:

> Common assessment would normally therefore be undertaken before a decision about referral to social services is made.

Social care workers will be expected to use this framework but it is clear that this will not replace the more in depth assessment for children in greater need. The Scottish Executive has established a multi-agency working group to prepare an assessment framework for use by all those working with children: the Integrated Assessment Framework.

Empowering the family

It is endemic to social work that family members should participate in determining the direction of change. What is happening in the family may belie the wishes of family members and undermine the needs of some or all. Neither parents nor children may be able to express or live out their wishes. Social workers seek to enable family members to identify both what they want and the extent to which they are able, with or without help, to achieve those ends. They will discuss ways of achieving those things that the family cannot currently achieve and develop plans for achieving them. In these ways they begin to enable and empower families. The extent to which they can develop relationships of trust with family members will determine how far family aims, capacities and plans are identified and developed.

Dealing with conflicting needs and wishes

While this partnership approach is at the heart of social work, there is a further responsibility to ensure that the needs of those who are most vulnerable in the situation are not neglected to their detriment. In families it is the children to whom social workers owe the greater duty of care. There may be tensions between children's needs and wishes, parents' needs and wishes, the views and wishes of the wider family, of the community, other professionals, and with the requirements of the law, regulation and procedure.

Social workers must take all of this into account. Consulting with others they must judge what action should be taken in the best interests of the children, though where there is a dispute with parents it will be the children's hearing tribunal that makes the 'final' decision. The protective role is always at the forefront of social work considerations. The need for immediate protective action may appear to frustrate the family's goals. It is in such areas of social control that conflict between perspectives about the need for social work intervention and what it should be about is most apparent.

If the assessment is that the child's need for protection requires removal from its parent(s) the resulting action may indeed frustrate the family's goals in the long, as well as the short, term. The requirement for formal processes to be followed and the work entailed often divert the social worker's time, attention and efforts away from the work needed to enable the parents to meet their support goals. The action may also break any relationship of trust between a particular social worker and parent(s) and destroy any possibility of working together on a longerterm goal. Nonetheless, the way social workers conduct their business can make a difference. Looking at families' involvement in child protection Thoburn et al found that parents and children most valued being cared about as individuals, with both strengths and weaknesses.

Achieving change, meeting goals: direct and indirect work

If the assessment allows for the child to remain in the care of parent(s) the social worker may be become principal person enabling the parents to achieve their goals. The social worker's skills in counselling may help the parent(s) identify why they are not attaining their goals, what they need to do to meet their own and their child's needs. The social worker may develop and implement a programme of work with the parent(s) or child, negotiate for another professional to undertake a programme of work with parent(s) or child or negotiate access to day care, respite care, welfare benefits, any or all of which may relieve stress or exhaustion. The social worker works as therapist and advocate or broker. Again, the social worker's role can be the necessary element in making a package of services successful:

> '...there should always be a key worker who will offer continuity and a supportive or therapeutic relationship as well as marshalling and coordinating the packages of help and monitoring the child's wellbeing... If this element of continuity is in place our study suggests that additional workers can with advantage be brought in alongside the key worker to provide short term specialist assessment or therapeutic services...'
>
> [But in tertiary prevention it] appears important to combine it [social network interventions] with intensive casework, advocacy and case management...particularly in the early stages of relationshipbuilding with families.

As advocates, negotiators or brokers social workers have to understand the needs of the family members and have knowledge about services, their purpose, qualities, accessibility and availability. Social workers must be able to put a convincing case to the service provider and provide relevant and sufficient information for the provider to make an informed decision. For the provider to have to collect information to make a full reassessment of the need for the service would be inefficient and unhelpful to the user. As before, having obtained a service for the user, the social worker is involved in assessment, measuring the progress being made towards change and the effect of the process and any change on the overall situation for the family.

The social worker's protective role may extend to promoting the particular needs of vulnerable children and families in the context of services designed for the less vulnerable. While the change to greater teamwork and integrated assessments places more equal responsibilities on the range of professions and agencies, at least for the time being, social work needs to champion those who cannot speak up for themselves or who alienate themselves through disruptive behaviour or poor social skills.

Social workers may take a direct role with children, including helping them to come to terms with transitions in their lives brought about by parent's inability to continue caring for them, on account of, for example, of illness or substance abuse. They may counsel young carers helping them to work out the extent of the care they can give and what they personally need to do in the absence of sufficient support for the parent/s needs.

Social workers may also help children and parents to maintain any changes made. Continued support of this kind may attract criticism as encouraging dependency but practice experience has indicated that failing to provide such support may reduce the return on substantial investment of social work resources. A complementary strategy is to assist and encourage families in developing wider family and social networks.

Social Work Intervention

Because of the social and political context for social work with children and families the process of social work intervention described above may easily be distorted by an assumption that care and expertise lie outside the family. And, despite much broader policy and aspirations for social work with children and their parents, the major preoccupation of statutory social work departments appears to be with protecting children from abuse and neglect and protecting others from abuse by children and young people. Examination of what happens in practice indicates that attention and effort are driven towards children living in the most difficult circumstances. Sometimes even they have to wait for intervention. Examples of this are described in For Scotland's Children. The control functions mandated by the state take precedence.

Children can be clear about what they need – a focus on them as individuals; response without having to repeat their story; respect; and promises delivered. There is professional and political acknowledgement that a wide variety of situations make children and their parents vulnerable. Social work is undertaken in a variety of voluntary and independent organisations – small and large. It is not confined to the statutory sector.

Social work skills and processes outlined above:

- recognising and describing the problem
- assessing the situation
- empowering the family
- enabling family members to identify both what they want and how they can best achieve those ends
- counselling
- negotiating access to information, advice and services
- acting as therapist and advocate or broker
- championing those who cannot speak up for themselves can be valuable to any children and

families involved in the childhood journey to independence, adulthood and citizenship.

This indicates clear benefits to the children, their families and the wider community. Social work is not always so bold in setting out its positive impact. And, as noted, it is often impossible to disentangle the effect of social work from the other factors at work in families' lives.

It is encouraging to record and be involved in social work that has tangible impacts, that change lives for the better, measured in terms of outcomes set down in public policy. Social work has value also in working alongside people who want change, results and improvement and for whom none comes. In children and families work this may be most easily understood, and acceptable, in situations in which parents are supported in caring for severely disabled or terminally ill children; or with parents whose children are placed for adoption against their will. The changes may not fit the desired outcomes for children but may make an important but less tangible difference to the quality of life of all concerned.

This aspect of social work, supporting and being alongside people whose lives are painful, is more controversial in other aspects of children and families work. There are many situations in which the obstacles to the state's objectives for the child being met appear to emanate from the parents' inability or unwillingness to provide the desired environment and care. Removal may be the societal response; in all children and family work ultimately, and rightly, the overriding principle is that the welfare of the child is paramount. But there is no guarantee that alternative care, in the wider family, or in family or residential placement, will meet the needs of the child.

Social work is needed to point out the difficulties, weigh up the choices, and stay with the situation, listening and supporting, preventing deterioration where possible and organising compensatory experiences for the child. In these situations social work is also needed to be alert to the signals of possibilities for positive and negative change, to keep alert to the whole picture, while other professionals address more discrete needs. Were social work to be seen as non-threatening, available to all at the behest of the user and to meet the requirements of the user, social work by invitation rather than social work intervention, parents and children might also value social work's 'whole person/whole situation' approach.

Families might be readier to accept the support and encouragement of social work to fight or withstand obstacles outside their and social work's control, for example, separation from the wider family, poor housing, poverty, intolerance, complex systems and procedures. Social work's contribution may again be difficult to measure but significantly affect the quality of life of the whole family. Families might also be prepared to explore what social work has to offer in intra and interpersonal issues, without compulsion.

Conflicts and tensions

Social work and much of the financial resource for it get their legitimacy from legislation. Social work with children and families is highly regulated and increasingly all sectors are brought within the statutory frame. This seems to have resulted in an approach/attitude that legitimises only that work which is in line with objectives and targets. The state wants children to flourish; so do parents. Parents and children are individuals; some may not have the capacity to meet targets. Social work bears the burden of working with the individual within the context of a framework for the many. It is needed to hold the balance.

Children and parents may flourish at different rates. They may flourish in response to different stimuli and settings. They need confidence and a safe environment. Social work is required to help to prevent tragedies. Social work is needed to give confidence to families to flourish and to the state to be safe.

There is an inherent tension in social work with children and parents between the needs and wishes of the parents and the needs and wishes of the child. Most usually the needs and wishes of the child are met through the agency of parents. Thus social work has to promote parental needs for the sake of the children but may need to abandon them to maintain the primacy of the child's welfare. The consequences of getting the balance wrong in either direction expose both children and parents to suffering and pain.

Social work is dependent on engaging its service users. This involves listening and understanding and responding to what is heard.

Social Work with Adults of Working Age and Older People

A good deal of work has gone on in Scotland in recent years to review and develop policy for social work services to the adult client groups. Following 'Aiming for Excellence – Modernising Social Work Services in Scotland', there has been a focus on policies to promote empowerment and inclusion, strengthen safeguards for vulnerable adults and those lacking capacity, develop more integrated approaches to assessment and service delivery, and build the capacity of communities to support individuals and families and promote well-being.

The thrust of these policies is generally consistent with evidence from research and policy-making elsewhere in the UK on adult protection, social and community inclusion, personalisation, empowerment and evidence-based practice. The Scottish Social Services Council and other Scottish institutions have worked alongside their counterparts in the rest of the UK on the workforce, education and training implications of these policies, particularly as they affect social work and social workers.

Limitations of the Client Group Approach

Much legislation and policy, both pre- and post-devolution, uses traditional definitions of client-groups – children and young people, disabled people, people with learning disabilities, with mental health problems, with problems of alcohol and drug misuse, and older people. It is questionable, for several reasons, how useful these groupings will be as the 21st century proceeds.

Many people in the adult groups have a range and variety of physical, sensory, mental health, substance misuse and/ or learning difficulties, in different mixes, which interact with each other and with acute and chronic health conditions including HIV/AIDS to produce a wide diversity of obstacles to ordinary living, social inclusion and the exercise of their human and civil rights. The same conditions and combinations affect the lives of children, young people and their families, and of people over 60 or 65. Children in need or at risk are often living in families, or with other adults, where effective parenting is impaired by the adults' problems of mental health, substance misuse, intellectual or social impairment, or chronic ill-health. So-called 'young carers' are affected in different ways by the support they need to give to parents with the various impairments, and in some instances parents' uncontrolled substance misuse or acute mental illness may pose a serious threat to the children's safety and well-being.

The term 'older people' can encompass two complete generations, as retirement takes place between 50 and 70 or more, and the numbers living into their 90s and beyond grow rapidly. Ageing makes people increasingly prone to the effects of physical and sensory impairments, medical conditions associated with physical deterioration, falls and other accidents, depression, functional mental illness and various forms of dementia. Adults with learning difficulties, including some with multiple impairments, are increasingly living into old age. Occasional or chronic substance misuse is also likely to be a growing problem amongst older people.

Various terms and sub-divisions are in use, such as 3rd Age and 4th Age, 'sundowners' and 'frail elderly people', to distinguish the relatively active, unimpaired and independent from those with often multiple physical, sensory, mental health and psychological problems who require treatment and support from a variety of agencies and other sources. In reality the line between relative independence and complete dependency is a spectrum with a multitude of stages, and people move along it in different and highly individual patterns.

Many 'older people' are contributing to the community in various ways as carers and minding grandchildren, in paid employment, as volunteers and in voluntary organisations, as councillors at different levels of local government. The loss of a spouse, onset or discovery of severe illness, a fall and loss of confidence, or being victim of a burglary, can all produce an abrupt shift towards greater dependency. Conversely, successful treatment or effective aids to alleviate a mobility or sensory problem, moving to manageable accommodation, gaining a valued role or establishing a new relationship, can all restore confidence and self-esteem and enable people to regain different degrees of independence.

Socio-Economic Factors

All the groups for whom social work intervention is likely to be needed are also more subject than most to a range of social and economic problems and barriers. A major factor is chronic poverty, often associated with unemployment or enforced retirement, long-term dependence on social security benefits, being the adult or a child in single parent families, and living in old age with inadequate pension provision. Poverty often goes hand in hand with other disadvantages and obstacles such as poor educational and employment opportunities, inadequate housing, living in deprived and run-down neighbourhoods, limited transport facilities, and lack of access to public services and commercial opportunities.

People's problems are exacerbated by the interaction between these socioeconomic factors and their individual impairments and family situations. Many forms of disability generate additional costs to the individual for elements of everyday living. Unemployment levels are very high among disabled people and those with long-term mental health problems, who are also subject to stigma and prejudice on the part of employers. People without jobs and dependent on benefits find it hard to access credit. Poor children, those growing up in oneparent families and children in the public care suffer serious educational disadvantage, which in turn impairs their job prospects in later life. Ill-adapted and hard-to-heat housing has an adverse effect on older people's health and wellbeing, and social isolation made worse by mobility and transport problems can undermine their mental health.

Need for Social work Intervention with Adults

From the individual's point of view, the need for social work intervention is likely to arise if they are unable, without it, to achieve outcomes they are seeking for themselves and their families. For adults of working age and older people, these outcomes may be in one or more of the following areas:

— *Exercise of Choice and Control* – fully exercising human and civil rights and equal opportunities, maintaining or regaining maximum independence, managing risks inherent in ordinary life, being able to access information and choose and control support arrangements, being free from discrimination, harassment, neglect, exploitation or abuse.

— *Economic Well-being* - access to income and resources, from employment, pension, benefits and other sources, sufficient for a good diet, accommodation, heating, communications, participation in family and community life, and to meet costs arising from specific individual needs.

— *Improved Quality of Life* – suitable and convenient accommodation, safety and security at home and outside, access to transport, leisure, social activities, life long learning and universal, public and commercial services, ability to secure appropriate levels and preferred forms of support and personal care when required

— *Making a Positive Contribution* – engaging in education and training to reach full potential, having access to work appropriate to individual's abilities, active participant in the community through employment, voluntary and public service opportunities, involvement in local activities including participation in developing support service policy, decision making, provision and practice.

— *Improved Health* - Maintaining good physical, emotional and mental health, personal dignity and respect, with opportunities for physical activity and access to appropriate treatment and to support in managing long term conditions independently, keeping clean and comfortable in a chosen environment.

In response to these desired outcomes, the specific contribution of social work is to adopt a holistic approach to understanding the needs and difficulties of individuals and families in their social context, and to help them develop the solutions and achieve the outcomes that best fit their strengths, aspirations and preferences. This requires skills in working with and across a range of agencies and disciplines, adherence to a strong value base in a range of situations where solutions are not prescribed, the capacity to address conflicts of interest between individuals and between an individual or family and wider society, and the ability to exercise control when required within legal and professional frameworks with the minimum of damage to the individual's integrity. It also requires a range of personal qualities:

— the capacity to tolerate uncertainty and anxiety and not to close down options prematurely
— a mature, unthreatened sense of their own identity
— good emotional intelligence and an ability to establish relationships in situations of challenge and risk
— clarity in assessing and responding to situations involving complex relationships and risks
— flexibility in analysing human situations and developing creative solutions
— the intellectual curiosity to stay up-to-date and develop a broad understanding of people and their circumstances

- acceptance of multiple, sometimes competing accountabilities.

These requirements are common to working with children, adults and families, and reflect the reality that most children live with one or more parents or other adults, and that both the children and/or the adults involved are more likely than most families to experience difficulties stemming from the health or social problems listed. They support the model found in a number of other professions, where initial training and qualification is common and specialisation in training and practice takes place at the post-qualifying stage.

Most of the outcomes sought through social work intervention are common to work with adults of working age and with older people. Social work with adults entails:

- encouraging all professionals involved to take and keep taking an allround view from the person's perspective
- working together with the person and others on strategies for their empowerment, independence and control of their own lives
- identifying the person's abilities, assets and potential for capacity-building, and enabling them to develop to the full
- assisting the person to explore and access alternative living situations, including those with the benefits of smart housing and housing-based support schemes
- assisting the person with their assessment of their support needs and preferred solutions, and with securing satisfactory arrangements
- where the person wishes, helping them to access direct payments and establish and manage support arrangements to their specifications

— assisting the person and their family through the transition to higher levels of support needs, whether through increased disability, ill-health or bereavement, or in order to access opportunities for independence and participation
— helping to resolve charging and payment issues in the user's interests
— supporting the person to access help with financial planning, budgeting, raising income and securing credit without being exploited
— supporting the person in exercising their human and civil rights, including rights to privacy, family life, freedom from enforced constraints
— intervening in complex partnership or family situations to resolve relationship problems, conflicts of interest and damaging interaction affecting physical and mental health
— ensuring, with maximum input from the individual, safeguards against exploitation, unnecessary constraint, neglect, domestic violence and abuse
— with the person, their family and others they trust, helping them avoid being or becoming an unacceptable risk to themselves or others
— within statutory frameworks, intervening to prevent the person becoming an unacceptable threat to others or themselves
— helping carers to maintain their support role in line with the person's preferences and their own wishes, without the carers suffering exploitation, damage to health, isolation or social exclusion, and avoiding over-protection or undue pressure on the person
— helping people with restricted capacity to protect their interests in relation to family members, neighbours and others who could take advantage

Additional elements in work with adults below retirement age (itself an increasingly flexible concept) would include:

- assisting the person and their family in the transitions from services for children and young people to those for adults, and the natural process of becoming fully adult and less dependent on parental care
- supporting the person to access remedial, further and higher educational to maximise their level of achievement and qualification
- supporting the person to access and benefit from professional and vocational training opportunities to equip them for jobs, including selfemployment, appropriate to their skills and abilities
- support the person to enter and maintain employment suitable to their abilities and expectations, and to develop satisfying and challenging careers in their chosen fields

Implications and Issues for Consideration

The issues for social workers and their managers and employers highlighted include

- managing the relationship between user preferences and society's expectation for control and protection
- the differences in social work with groups who are included, tolerable and tolerated by society, and those who are excluded or regarded as intolerable
- how far the social worker's role includes being the advocates and champions of outsiders and groups defined as 'too difficult'
- the social worker's remit for mediating between the whole person and the full range of supports and

services which may enable them to achieve the outcomes they seek

- the implications of dealing with the whole person in relation to their family, community and society, particularly where this involves competing or conflicting interests
- the tensions in working as professionals accountable to the people using their services, their regulatory body, employers allocating resources and setting targets, and government determining policy
- conflicts in the social worker's role when rationing scarce resources and applying eligibility criteria to exclude some with assessed needs
- how the social worker's focus on empowerment and enabling people to manage their own lives can be balanced with assessing and helping people to manage risk, and with responsibilities for adult and child protection
- identifying and extending 'the best available evidence' as a basis for social work practice
- recognising the human element in social work, in its dealings with weaknesses, mistakes and uncertainty

The Social Work Review may also wish to consider a wider set of issues with implications for some of the key stakeholders:

- Should social work become a mainstream, universal service available on request?
- What is the scope for developing existing and new staff roles and support systems to make the most effective use of the scarce and skilled resource social workers represent?
- Does social work require its own distinctive form of professionalism to support a person-centred, outcome-oriented social model of practice?

- What liabilities do employers carry for actively supporting the continuing learning and professional development of their social work staff?
- What routes are available to strengthen the engagement of education and research academics with the complex world of social work practice?
- What mechanisms would support a shared responsibility for developing and continuously updating the knowledge base for social work?
- Are there ways to avoid specialist team structures, geared to facilitate inter-agency working, creating additional boundaries and obstacles for people to overcome?
- How far is it possible to promote coherent government policies, integrated across departmental boundaries, which take account of the whole person in their family and social situation?

10

Social Work for Adolescence

Adolescence marks an important time in the process of human development, the passage between childhood and adulthood. It is a time of tremendous opportunity and promise, when young people begin to explore their burgeoning individuality and independence and begin to think critically about themselves and the world around them. They begin to adjust and adapt to the profound biological, psychological, and social changes and challenges that are by-products of adolescence.

The manner in which adolescents navigate these changes and challenges is largely a function of interactions—both positive and negative—with families, communities, and the larger social environment. The health and well-being of our young people (and the adults they will become) are critically affected by their experiences during this developmental milestone.

Healthy adolescent development depends on safe and supportive environments that are free from violence and from the risks of physical, mental, and emotional harm environments that provide opportunities for youths to build strong and meaningful connections with their families, their schools, and their communities. Adolescents greatly benefit from engagement in activities in which their value is demonstrated and affirmed and their inherent talents, capabilities, and strengths are enhanced. Social environments that are inclusive and accepting of diversity encourage all youths to feel good about and value themselves and others around them. Equitable access to quality education, health care, employment opportunities, and social supports also are essential for ensuring positive outcomes for youths.

Most young people are able to navigate these adolescent years successfully with the support of caring families and communities. Far too many youths, however, experience significant challenges during this time that impede their ability to move successfully into adulthood. The healthy development of adolescents is thwarted by the invasion of drugs and violence into homes, schools, and social environments. Impoverished conditions may offer limited or no access to basic needs and present barriers for youths and their families. These barriers prevent access to adequate health care and social services, education, employment opportunities, housing, and nutrition. Youths also may be exposed to violence, abuse, bullying, harassment, and neglect in their homes, schools, and communities.

Some youths may experience alienation, disenfranchisement, and discrimination from the families, communities, and social institutions charged with supporting their development. Youths with severe health and mental health problems or disabilities, runaway and homeless youths, youths in foster care or juvenile justice systems, and gay, lesbian, bisexual, and transgender adolescents often experience alienation. These social conditions leave young people more vulnerable to health-damaging behaviors such as substance abuse, delinquent activities, unprotected sexual activity, and mental health pathology.

Social workers understand that everyone—individuals, communities, and society as a whole—reaps the benefits from investments in helping our young people achieve optimal physical and mental health. Social workers provide essential services in the environments, communities, and social systems that affect the lives of youths. To meet the needs of young people, it is important for social workers to demonstrate a fundamental knowledge and understanding of adolescent development and the critical role of biopsychosocial systems.

Standards for the Practice of Social Work with Adolescents

Standard 1. Knowledge of Adolescent Development

Social workers shall demonstrate knowledge and understanding of adolescent development. Essential areas of knowledge and understanding about positive adolescent development include:

- human growth and behavior, including developmental stages, human needs, motivations, feelings, behaviors, activities of children and youths, and cultural differences
- the role of adolescence in individuals' social, physical, emotional, and sexual growth, including adolescents' striving for and ambivalence about independence, competence, achievement, personal identity, and sexuality
- the critical role of education in healthy adolescent development and the barriers to a successful educational experience
- the necessity to recognise the needs of adolescent development
- the impact of substance abuse and violence on adolescents' development and on their families

- the family, school, community, and cultural process for allowing and helping adolescents become independent
- the importance of opportunities for adolescents to establish positive relationships with open expression of thoughts and feelings with family members, peers, and role models such as teachers, clergy, and sports team coaches
- the significance of adolescents' steps in establishing an identity, which may include a natural form of rebelliousness and rejection of authority.

Standard 2. Assessment

Social workers shall demonstrate an ability to assess adolescent services, including access to social institutions and community-based resources that provide services for adolescents and their families, and shall advocate for the development of needed resources.

Social workers shall possess the following fundamental knowledge and skills to work effectively with adolescents and their families:

- the history and development of social work and its person-in-environment perspective
- the theory, principles, and methods of social work, including casework, group work, community organisation, administration, supervision, planning, and research
- the influence of cultural beliefs, background, lifestyles, and ethnicity
- the interrelationships among the individual and the family, the group, the neighborhood, the community, and social systems

- the purpose, structure, legal mandates, and services provided by public and voluntary social welfare, child welfare, and youth services agencies; schools; and health, mental health, juvenile justice, and law enforcement organisations
- an ability to coordinate with other professionals and community organisations and advocate for their involvement on behalf of youths
- the political and economic factors affecting adolescents, their families, and their communities
- multidisciplinary and team approaches for working with children and youths, and the contributions from biomedical, psychological, social sciences, legal, educational, law enforcement, and other disciplines
- opportunities available to adolescents for training to increase job-related skills
- an understanding of the importance of working with adolescents in the environments in which they feel comfortable, including nontraditional environments
- familiarity with groups who provide peer education and improve youths' decision making and leadership skills
- understanding of and ability to develop a case plan jointly with youths and their families
- an understanding of how to develop programs that provide comprehensive services to adolescents to prevent fragmentation
- an understanding of how to develop programs that will increase the likelihood that youths will use available services for the range of issues that affect adolescents (for example, reproductive health, HIV/AIDS and other STIs, violence, and abuse).

Standard 3. Knowledge of Family Dynamics

Social workers shall demonstrate knowledge and understanding of family dynamics and systems theory. *Families* as two or more people who consider themselves "family" and who assume obligations, functions, and responsibilities generally essential to healthy family life. Essential areas of knowledge about family dynamics include

- family dynamics in traditional and nontraditional families, including two-parent, single-parent, and foster and adoptive families and unrelated individuals living together as a family, and acceptance and understanding of such family constellations
- the impact of adolescents' parents' growth experiences, attitudes, and behaviors and culturally relevant ways for parents to ask for help
- an understanding of how to bring about changes in family functioning
- the concept of family culture, including the role of the family in meeting the changing physical, mental, spiritual, and emotional needs of adolescents
- cultural attitudes toward the responsibilities of each family member
- the impact of impairment and disability, including mental and emotional disabilities, chemical dependency, and abusive conditions on positive adolescent development and family dynamics
- an understanding of changing parental roles and the diversity among those roles
- the impact of economic, social, and cultural conditions on parental ability to meet family responsibilities.

Standard 4. Cultural Competence

Social workers shall demonstrate culturally competent service delivery. The increasingly diverse population in the United States requires that social workers raise their awareness and appreciation of cultural differences. They must develop competencies that include heightened self-awareness, knowledge, and practice skills.

Culturally competent social workers should be knowledgeable about the deleterious effects of racism, sexism, ageism, heterosexism or homophobia, anti-Semitism, ethnocentrism, classism, and disability-based discrimination on adolescents' lives and about the need to advocate for and with adolescents. Social workers must recognise racial, ethnic, gender, and cultural differences that may be interpreted as barriers and develop strategies and skills to ameliorate such barriers.

Standard 5. Self-Empowerment of Adolescents

Social workers shall help adolescents achieve selfempowerment. Social workers should demonstrate the necessary knowledge and skills to ensure the participation of adolescents in decisions about the programs and services designed to meet their needs. This includes

- encouraging youths and their families to be active participants in their case planning and service delivery
- developing adolescent leaders to provide peer support to other adolescents and supporting their efforts
- advocating for youth positions and roles of influence on agency boards or committees and providing training for youths to develop the skills needed to improve existing services and develop necessary services

- working with youths and their families to help them assume responsibility for following through on a plan of action and for securing and using planned services
- providing or brokering the training and support to help youths develop independent living skills.

Standard 6. Understanding Adolescents' Needs

Social workers shall advocate for an understanding of the needs of adolescents and for resources and cooperation among professionals and agencies to meet those needs. Social workers who work with adolescents should respect and work to strengthen the many protective factors that are sometimes overlooked or ignored. Appropriate and effective work with adolescents requires an understanding of the developmental skills and tasks characteristic of the age, an awareness of the psychosocial and emotional phases of adolescence, and clinical knowledge of inappropriate behavior and symptoms of mental illness or stress. Social workers should be aware that adolescents' behaviors and attitudes may provoke ambivalent or negative feelings in those who work with this age group.

Social workers need to be aware of adolescents' multidimensional lives, regardless of service focus. This includes the family, siblings, extended family, individuals with whom the adolescent may reside, peer group, friends of the opposite sex, religious affiliation, physical and mental health, cultural and economic facts, refugee status, discrimination experiences, and exposure to violence in the community or family or from war experiences. In advocating for adolescents, social workers must work to ensure that

- continuing education is available for providers, professionals, and families of adolescents to develop skills and a knowledge base, to acknowledge and enhance adolescent protective and resilient factors, and to strengthen empowerment capacities and decision-making skills

- community services are responsive to the mental health, physical, medical, educational, vocational and occupational training, housing, and other needs of adolescents as articulated by adolescents and their families
- agencies provide opportunities for staff to recognise and take appropriate actions to resolve their own biases, fears, or antipathy about behaviors exhibited by adolescent clients
- policies and programs adjust, change, or accommodate to meet the needs of adolescents in different settings and with different disabilities or mental or physical limitations
- opportunities are provided for adolescents to discuss, learn about, and appreciate the uniqueness of different cultures, personalities, and interactions
- knowledge is increased about medical and substance abuse issues, methods of fostering healthy attitudes, interventions, and behavior toward drug use among targeted youths
- improved school connections are encouraged to improve academic performance, school attendance and behavior, and attitudes toward learning and achievement
- opportunities for strong relationships with adults and peers for positive and supportive interaction are available
- information about model programs for prevention and treatment is available

- information is disseminated on the effects of alcohol, substance abuse, domestic and dating violence, and HIV/AIDS to families and communities
- information, news, and updates about pressures on adolescents from different cultures, income levels, and ethnic groups are routinely provided
- opportunities to identify and address risk-taking behavior are available in community forums and parent groups, as well as with educators, juvenile justice staff, and law enforcement officials
- opportunities for collaboration among community, religious, and athletic groups are supported
- opportunities exist to recognise adolescent achievements.

Standard 7. Multidisciplinary Case Consultation

Social workers shall participate in multidisciplinary case consultation across agencies that provide services to adolescents. To develop the most appropriate case plan with adolescents and their families, social workers must consult with other individuals, professionals, and organisations who work with adolescents without violating confidentiality. Such consultation should include

- joint assessment of youths' presenting problems, family strengths, and risk factors
- joint assessment of the need for available services and interventions
- individual evaluations of adolescents' progress and joint consultation following the evaluations
- joint appraisal of youths' successes and failures when the cases are closed and assessment of alternatives that were available for the case plan

— involving adolescents and their families in care planning

Standard 8. Confidentiality

Social workers shall maintain adequate safeguards for privacy and confidentiality in their relationships with youths. Respect for the client as a person and for his or her right to privacy underlies the social worker– client relationship. Except for federal, state, or local legal and other overriding requirements, the social worker will share information only with the informed and signed consent of the youth, the family, or both. Although assurance of confidentiality enhances the relationship and the willingness of the youth to develop and adhere to a case plan, the youth should be advised that there are circumstances in which confidentiality cannot be maintained. These situations may include

— suspicion of child abuse or neglect, which requires that appropriate authorities be notified

— suspicion of danger to the youth or to others. In all such situations, the social worker shall advise the youth of the exceptions to confidentiality and privilege, shall be prepared to share with the youth the information that is being reported, and shall appropriately address the feelings evoked.

Standard 9. Work Environment

Social workers shall assume an active role in contributing to the improvement and quality of the work environment, agency policies and practices with clients, and their own professional development.

Social workers are responsible, in part, for their own empowerment as staff of the organisations in which they work. As integral members of an agency, social workers who work with adolescents are to conform to the mission and expectations established by that agency. Social workers should

- initiate action to ensure that agency policies and practices establish reasonable expectations that allow them to perform their jobs most effectively
- work for constructive change so that the work environment allows them to meet youths' needs and derive the support needed to do so
- be responsible for remaining prepared for their duties in the provision of social work services by seeking relevant continuing education and training programs and competent supervision
- assume responsibility for helping their colleagues by sharing their knowledge and skills
- document the need for changes in agency policy, practices, continuing education, and training and discuss the information with agency management.

Standard 10. Advocacy

Social work administrators in youth services agencies shall advocate for an increased understanding of the needs of youths, policy changes and adequate resources to enable social workers to meet those needs, and appropriate working conditions for all workers.

To fulfill this standard, the social work administrator is expected to

- solicit and allocate program funds and resources sufficient to respond to emergency, short-term, and longer-term needs of youths and their families
- provide opportunities for youths to participate in the design and implementation of service programs
- provide transportation and individual telephone lines to ensure that social work staff may help

youths and their families obtain needed services that will support family functioning or contribute to the adolescent's preparation for independence

- employ sufficient staff to work with all clients and their families
- establish and disseminate reasonable work loads for staff
- provide appropriate and adequate supervision and opportunities for multidisciplinary consultation services
- provide opportunities and time for staff development and continuing education on the basis of an agency assessment of training needs
- establish a salary schedule that is appropriate with regard to the social worker's education, work experience, and job responsibilities
- provide liability protection for the agency and staff
- advocate for public policies on the local, state, and national levels that support the goals and client population of the agency
- ensure appropriate space and working environment for social work staff to work and for privacy to maintain confidentiality.

Standard 11. Policies for Effective Practice

Social work administrators in youth services agencies shall establish the environment, policies, procedures, and guidelines necessary for effective social work practice with adolescents. The social work administrator is responsible for providing a supportive work environment that ensures that the staff concerns are addressed within the agency and with cooperating agencies that serve the same adolescent population. The administrator is also responsible for ensuring that the agency is responsive to the needs of the youths and their families. The policies and procedures should include:

- personnel and recruitment policies to ensure a diverse staff and pluralism in the agency
- public education materials and participation in public discussions to solicit public support for the goals of the program
- operational policies and procedures for dealing with specific issues such as suspected parental abuse, abuse in a previous residential setting, treatment of substance abuse problems, and treatment of HIV/AIDS and other STIs
- interagency agreements to ensure collaboration among those who serve the same adolescent population
- establishment of a safe and secure working environment, with measures to protect staff from violent youths and family members and from violence in the surrounding area
- systematic administrative and evaluative reviews of the program and opportunities for board members (including youths) and staff to participate in the development of program policies
- hiring professional social work staff with bachelor of social work or master of social work degrees from accredited programs, with demonstrated work skills, and with characteristics that reflect the ethnic composition of the clientele served by the agency
- clearly written job descriptions and affirmative action and other personnel policies, including grievance procedures
- program evaluation by youths and their families, funding sources, and other community agencies and referral sources.

11

Long-term Social Work Strategies

Long-term care is an increasingly important and rapidly changing component of today's social services delivery system. The need for long-term care services is expected to increase dramatically in the United States as the population ages. Changing demographics have continued to affect the demand for long-term care services and the availability of social workers to provide care to the most vulnerable members of our society. As the number of individuals in need of long-term care services rises, new issues surrounding staffing, family involvement, quality of life, the role of spirituality, end-of-life care, medical management, program development, and overall service delivery are emerging.

The principal components of social work services in long-term care settings are designed to provide assessment, treatment, rehabilitation, and supportive care, and to preserve and enhance social functioning. Service provision requires a unique combination of physical, psychological, and social interventions and family support, the goal of which is to promote an optimal level of psychological, physical, and social functioning.

There have been significant changes in the manner in which long-term care services are delivered across the long-term care spectrum. Long-term care services and programs have evolved into a variety of institutional and noninstitutional modalities. Because long-term care encompasses a wide array of services, many definitions of long-term care exist. The need for long-term care services most often arises among older people, but some people need long-term care services because of physical, mental, or developmental limitations that occur at birth or at any point across the life span. Long-term care services can be provided in a person's own home, in the community, or in a facility. However, even with changing patterns of care, long-term care facilities, as temporary or permanent providers of care, are still a major resource for those who receive social work services in this country.

Guiding Principles

Social work services in long-term care settings focus on several key areas, including the social and emotional impact of physical or mental illness or disability, the preservation and enhancement of physical and social functioning, the promotion of the conditions essential to ensure maximum benefits from long-term health care services, the prevention of physical and mental illness and increased disability, and the promotion and maintenance of physical and mental health and an optimal quality of life.

Objectives include the following:

- providing direct social services to residents and their families by professionally trained social workers
- assisting residents and families to use and receive maximum benefit from the facility and community-based social and health resources on a continuum throughout the stay of each resident
- strengthening communications among residents, families, and the program or facility staff

- assisting the facility to achieve and maintain a therapeutic environment essential to the optimal quality of life and independent functioning of each resident and to provide for maximum participation of residents in planning activities and policies
- promoting facility–community interaction by encouraging community involvement in the facility along with resident and staff involvement in the community, developing linkages with a wide range of community resources, and participating in the assessment of and the need for planning related to other long-term social and health care resources.

Standards for Social Work Services in Long-Term Care Facilities

Standard 1. Ethics and Values

Social workers in long-term care facilities shall demonstrate a commitment to the values and ethics of the social work profession, emphasizing resident empowerment and self-determination.

Social workers shall demonstrate a recognition of basic human rights, including the right of residents to receive an optimal level of social services and medical care. With the recognition that change in long-term care settings is constant, social workers shall remain current by regularly evaluating and contributing to social work theory, policy, and practice. Social workers have a responsibility to know and comply with federal, state, and local legislation, regulations, and policies.

Standard 2. Service Plan

The long-term care facility shall maintain a written plan for defining social work services designed to ensure their availability to all residents and their families. The plan for social work services shall be guided by a written statement of philosophy, objectives, and policies.

An organised department under the leadership of a social work director is the preferable approach to providing social work services in long-term care facilities. The plan shall ensure that a professionally directed program will be provided. The plan shall document the philosophy, objectives, goals, policies, procedures, and scope of services provided. The plan shall provide for access to services for all residents and for prospective residents from preadmission until discharge or end-of-life. All services and programs shall be directed toward the following: creating a therapeutic environment to promote independent functioning; maintaining residents at or restoring residents to an optimal level of functioning; providing for the highest level of well-being; and allowing for maximum participation by the resident, the family, and staff involved with residents' care. The plan shall include, but not necessarily be limited to, the following:

- assurance of the selection of appropriately trained, educated, and licensed or credentialed social work staff
- communication and collaboration with the care plan team and others involved with residents' care
- collaboration with colleagues, community agencies, volunteers, and consultants
- development and implementation of services and special programs
- compliance with laws and regulations mandated by federal, state, and local governing bodies
- requirements for professional development and continuing education of social work staff

- maintenance of residents' medical records and reports mandated by federal, state, and local laws and the facility.

The social work director, in collaboration with other clinical and administrative representatives, is responsible for ensuring that the social work plan is implemented. The plan of the social work department shall provide procedures to ensure that all federal, state, and local laws are implemented and adhered to and shall be consistent with the facility's policies and regulations.

Standard 3. Responsibilities of Social Work Department

The social work director shall carry primary responsibility for social work services, including the development of organisational plans and administrative policies and procedures and coordination of services.

The social work director's responsibilities may include the following:

- development and implementation of all social health programs in the setting
- participation in budget planning, defining space and material requirements, and establishing qualifications and staffing patterns of social work personnel to ensure that appropriate and adequate services are provided consistent with stated goals and objectives
- implementation and oversight of procedures to ensure that adequate documentation of social work services is provided in each resident's medical record and that legal, ethical, and professional standards are observed in written recordings
- establishment and administration of a social work program that provides high-quality care and services reflective of professional standards of practice and in compliance with all federal, state, and local laws

- establishment and administration of quality assurance procedures and modification of these procedures where appropriate
- encouraging participation where appropriate in the education of social work interns, as well as other health care personnel and students and in the development, implementation, and review of research in which social workers can contribute
- ensuring that social work staff are knowledgeable about residents' rights in accordance with all federal, state, and local laws.

Standard 4. Program Functions

The functions of the social work program shall include, but not be limited to, direct services to residents, families, and other individuals involved with residents' care; advocacy; care planning, discharge planning and documentation; participation in policy and program planning; quality improvement; staff education pertaining to social services; liaison to the community; and consultation to other staff members.

Social work services should be designed to meet the biopsychosocial needs of residents, their families, and others involved with the residents' care and should be delivered in a manner that ensures confidentiality and cultural competence in accordance with professional standards. Specific social work functions may include, but are not be limited to, the following:

- preadmission services, including biopsychosocial assessments and participation in interdisciplinary evaluation of the individual's need for institutional care and preparation of the incoming resident
- identification of needs and coordination of services to ensure that the biopsychosocial needs of each resident are met

- participation in the development and reassessment, as needed, of individualised social service and interdisciplinary care plans designed to meet the biopsychosocial needs of each resident
- assisting residents and families in locating and using financial, legal, mental health, and other community resources
- provision of individual, family, and group services focused on the maintenance or enhancement of the resident's biopsychosocial functioning and understanding of the resident's placement and health status; services may include assistance with the following: concerns related to the resident's illness, disability, treatment, financial and medical decision making; placement and expectations of care; inter- or intrafacility transfers; interpersonal relationships; re-establishing community living; and coping with separation, loss, dying, and death
- advocacy of appropriate care and treatment of residents through the development and implementation of policies, and the education of residents, staff, and family regarding residents' rights, as well as consultation with the longterm care ombudsperson
- ensuring that health and mental health social work services are available to residents to assist with attaining or maintaining the highest practical mental and psychosocial well-being, while helping residents who display mental or psychosocial difficulty receive appropriate treatment and services
- acting as a resource to staff participating in behavioral interventions
- facilitating residents' safe integration into the community through interdisciplinary discharge planning and follow-up services

- participation in planning and policy development for the facility, including collaboration with other members of the staff in the identification of biopsychosocial, cultural, and environmental factors essential to the delivery of quality care to residents and families, participation in orientation of all new employees, and in-service training of facility personnel
- participation in resident and family council development, as needed or requested
- participation with medical personnel and facility staff in discussing with competent residents and families advance directives and financial powers of attorney; for incompetent residents, participation in discussions of guardianship and surrogate decision making
- orientation and supervision of volunteers
- contribution to the development of community resources by participating with community groups to initiate, plan, and carry out programs concerned with the health, mental health, and other welfare needs of the residents
- supervision of fieldwork for social work students in affiliation with an accredited school or program of social work
- participation in research and demonstration projects that may be conducted either independently or collaboratively.

Standard 5. Staffing

A sufficient number of appropriately trained licensed or credentialed and experienced social work and supportive personnel shall be available to plan, provide, evaluate, and modify all social work services.

The number and qualifications of the social work staff and the level of consultation needed shall be based on criteria related to the type, scope, and complexity of the social work program, the size of the facility, and the biopsychosocial needs and characteristics of the population served. All social work services shall be provided by social workers with experience in long-term care and a master's degree in social work or a baccalaureate degree in social work from an accredited school of social work.

All social work staff and consultants shall be licensed, certified, or registered as mandated by specific state licensing agency requirements in the state in which the social worker practices. The social work program shall have a sufficient number of appropriately trained or experienced support personnel to enable the provision of social work services that ensure each resident maintains or attains the highest practicable level of well-being.

Standard 6. Professional Development

To practice effectively, social workers in long-term care settings must remain knowledgeable about reforms in long-term care and best practice models in the social work profession.

Standard 7. Personnel Policies and Procedures

A written statement of the personnel policies and procedures of the facility for the social work department. Personnel policies that relate to the social work program and those of the facility shall be available to all staff. There shall be current written position descriptions and statement of qualifications within the specifications for each position. All staff, including social workers, shall have knowledge of and access to the personnel policies. These policies and procedures shall be periodically reviewed, communicated, and implemented.

Standard 8. Documentation

Documentation of social work services provided to residents, family members, and other individuals involved with the resident's care must be recorded in the medical record. Progress notes and other social work entries in the medical record shall be recorded to permit and encourage regular and ongoing communication with physicians and other professionals involved in the resident's care.

Entries by social work personnel shall include information related to the social and emotional functioning of the resident; relevant historical information regarding the resident and family and others involved with the resident's care; psychosocial assessments; the social work plan and specific goals; services provided and outcomes; and a summary of problems and goals attained, as well as reasons for nonattainment of goals.

Referrals to other agencies or resources should be documented in the resident's medical record and should include any ongoing follow-up or recommendations by an outside agency or individual. Notes shall be clear and concise. Progress notes, reports, and summaries of services shall be regularly recorded in the medical record and be consistent with all federal, state, and local legal and statutory, regulatory, and policy requirements and with the organisation's or facility's policies on reporting, maintenance of and access to records, and confidentiality.

Policies and procedures shall be developed and implemented to protect residents' rights to privacy, including confidentiality of records and procedures for release of information to individuals, and relevant community agencies.

Standard 9. Work Environment

There should be adequate budget, space, facilities, and equipment to fulfill the professional and administrative needs of the social work program. Offices of the social work staff must be readily accessible to residents, their families, and facility staff. They should provide privacy and confidentiality for individual, family, and group work; conferences; telephone calls; and documentation. Standard office equipment that adequately reflects current office technological needs should be provided.

Standard 10. Cultural Competence

Social workers shall provide residents and their families with social services in the context of multicultural understanding and competence. The increasingly diverse population in the United States requires that social workers raise their awareness and appreciation of cultural differences. Culturally competent social workers need to be knowledgeable about the deleterious effects of racism, sexism, ageism, heterosexism or homophobia, anti-Semitism, ethnocentrism, classism, and disability-based discrimination on residents' lives and the need to advocate for and with residents. Social workers must recognise racial, ethnic, and cultural differences that may be interpreted as barriers and develop strategies and skills that help ameliorate such barriers.

Standard 11. Interdisciplinary Collaboration

Social workers should be part of an interdisciplinary effort for the comprehensive delivery of longterm care services and should strive to enhance interdisciplinary and interorganisational cooperation. Social workers shall work in partnerships that include mutual respect, shared information, and effective communication.

As leaders and members of interdisciplinary teams, social workers must constantly be aware of the overall goals, objectives, and tasks of their practice area and interpret them to residents, families, and other relevant professions and organisations so that professional activities and competencies are maintained.

Social workers shall have a basic understanding of the missions and functions of other relevant professions and organisations that promote resident health, mental health, and well-being. Social workers shall be able to communicate, cooperate, and collaborate appropriately with professionals from different disciplines and agencies. The social work roles and responsibilities in long-term care shall be clearly delineated and communicated to other members of interdisciplinary teams.

As leaders and members of interdisciplinary teams, social workers must constantly be aware of the overall goals, objectives, and tasks of their practice area and interpret them to residents, families, and other relevant professions and organisations so that professional activities and competencies are maintained.

Social workers shall have a basic understanding of the missions and functions of other relevant professions and organisations that promote resident health, mental health, and well-being. Social workers shall be able to communicate, cooperate, and collaborate appropriately with professionals from different disciplines and agencies. The social work roles and responsibilities in long-term care shall be clearly delineated and communicated to other members of interdisciplinary teams.

12

Cross-cultural Social Work Practice

Time-honored practice theories and concepts are being vigorously challenged by a growing critique of the Eurocentric, hegemonic assumptions embedded in traditionally established practice. Calls for diversity-inclusive theorising and research have been met by unprecedented scholarly efforts directed towards conceptualising "cultural competence" and formulating practice guidelines for working with diverse populations.

A common theme in almost all conceptualisations of culturally competent practice is the need for practitioners to gain a deep and profound understanding of the "worldview" or "cultural frame of reference" of the client. Yet to be fully articulated, however, is a clear conceptual framework and attendant practice principles to guide the *process* of negotiating this kind of understanding in social work encounters.

Although empathy is identified in most classic and contemporary social work practice texts as a *sine qua non* of the helping relationship, the idea that practitioners can put themselves into the shoes of the other is increasingly seen as presumptuous. Devore and Schlesinger, for example, question the degree to which practitioners can empathically identify with clients whose life experiences may be "vastly different" than their own. Ibrahim questions whether traditional means of establishing and conveying empathy are appropriate with all cultural groups. The focus in traditional empathy theory on "feelings" rather than "cultural meanings" has been critiqued, as has the inattention to the cultural and sociopolitical context of human experience.

Further challenges to the concept of empathy have been raised on epistemological grounds. Intense insider/outsider debates, and the postmodern emphasis on the *otherness* of people's experience of themselves and the world have often left practitioners with paralysing doubts as to whether it is at all possible to empathically understand the culturally dissimilar "Other".

Paradoxically, while empathy faces serious challenges on conceptual grounds, renewed emphasis on the clinical importance of empathy has been sparked by mounting empirical evidence that "relationship" factors are more predictive of successful clinical outcome than treatment method or technique. The burgeoning helping alliance literature also underscores the importance of empathy as a central component in the formation of the alliance. Ironically, despite empathy's widely-accepted clinical significance, there has been surprisingly little research or theoretical development in this area in recent years, and few efforts have been directed towards reexamining empathy in the context of diversity. Fundamental questions lying at the heart of the social work profession await renewed theoretical and research attention, including:

- Is empathy still a useful concept for understanding the other's frame of reference?
- Are there other conceptual tools that can enlarge our understanding of how to create shared spaces for mutual understanding in cross-cultural dialogue?

— How can empathy be reconceptualised in ways that more fully attend to the multiple, intersecting diversities of participants in social work encounters?

Traditional Conceptualisations of Empathy

A broad consensus exists across disciplinary and theoretical perspectives that empathy is a fundamental feature of the helping process. It is widely considered to be one of the most basic skills required of the helping professional. Therapeutic alliance theorists place empathy "at the heart of the therapeutic relation and specifically of the therapeutic alliance". Within social work, empathy has been, and continues to be, identified as a foundational practice principle . What is noteworthy, however, is that current social work practice texts continue to rely on conceptualisations of empathy dating back several decades, primarily to Rogers, Truax and Carkhuff, and Perlman. There has been little theoretical development or research on empathy in recent years.

A variety of definitions and metaphors have been offered in the empathy literature over the decades, including: taking the role of the other; listening with the third ear; vicarious introspection; emotional knowing; entering imaginatively into the inner life of another; sensing and relating to the feelings underlying another's words and actions; attempting to see and experience things from another's perspective; entering into the feelings and experiences of another; and taking on the perspective of another.

Carl Rogers, arguably the most influential empathy theorist, defined empathy as "the perceiving of the internal frame of reference of another with accuracy...as if one were the other person but without ever losing the 'as if'condition. Rogers is perhaps best known for his famous and controversial assertion that empathy, warmth and genuineness are the necessary and sufficient "core conditions" for therapeutic change. For Rogers, empathic understanding was a particular type of deep, nonjudgmental understanding, distinct from that which comes from external frames.

While differing conceptualisations exist, three main "components" of empathy are routinely cited: cognitive, affective, and communicative. The question as to which component best captures the nature of empathy has become the source of a "central, recurrent, and seemingly intractable debate". A common strategy aimed at reconciling the affective-cognitive-communicative components of empathy has been to frame empathy as a series of stages or phases. Phase conceptualisations of empathy have been applied to many models of empathy skills training in which empathy is framed as a series of steps, stages, and degrees.

Limitations of Traditional Conceptualisations of Empathy

Several notable gaps and contestable assumptions severely constrain the continuing usefulness of traditional conceptualisations of empathy in the context of diversity.

Inattention to cultural meanings. Embedded in the empathy literature is the implicit assumption that empathy is a transcultural phenomenon which draws on "kindred feelings" shared by all human beings. Conspicuously absent is any discussion of the influence of cultural differences on empathic processes. Green challenges the universalist assumptions embedded in empathy theory, arguing that empathy as a technique in cross-cultural encounters is "inadequate" because it presumes an ability to enter into the sensibilities of another without first learning the context from which those sensibilities arise. He asserts that empathy needs to be "recast" from tuning in to feelings, to rigorous attention to the cultural meanings that clients and practitioners attach to behaviour, events, persons, and especially words.

Inattention to sociopolitical context. The emphasis in the literature on tuning in to the client's self-experience has not been accompanied by a corresponding emphasis on tuning in to the sociopolitical context of power and oppression that shapes the perspective and life experience of both clients and practitioners. Largely missing is a recognition that the helping relationship itself takes place in the context of racism, classism, sexism, heterosexism, ageism, ableism, and so on. The social location, and the associated power distribution of participants in the social work encounter has received scant attention in the empathy literature.

The positioning of the practitioner as expert knower. Influenced by its roots in a medical model, traditional conceptualisations of empathy typically position practitioners as "expert knowers" who supposedly understand their clients' lives better than the clients themselves. There is a preoccupation in the literature with "accurate" perception of the other's frame of reference, with little acknowledgment that the essential *otherness* of a human being can never be fully grasped. These assumptions have been strenuously critiqued by cross-cultural writers who stress the importance of approaching the client as "knower".

Uni-directional empathy. Most conceptualisations of empathy frame it as a "practitioner-offered" condition, ignoring the client's contribution to the process. Barrett-Lennard and Jordan are among the few who draw attention to the need for the *mutual* empathic involvement of both client and practitioner in negotiating understanding. The neglect of a dialogical dimension in traditional conceptualisations of empathy is a particular conceptual weakness.

Reductionist assumptions. A striking feature of the empathy literature is the focus on defining and operationalising empathy into a "scientific" construct that lends itself to empirical observation, quantitative investigation, and skills-training techniques. Most of the theorising and research on empathy is based on implicit empiricist assumptions that this complex, multidimensional phenomenon can be reduced to discreet, quantifiable elements. The practitioner's "subjectivity" is seen as an impediment that must be, and can be, controlled in order to gain objective, "accurate" understanding. The enormous effort directed to isolating, quantifying, measuring and sequentially ordering the components of empathy is in keeping with the reductionist demands of traditional scientific methods.

Multicultural Practice Theory

Multicultural practice theory not only offers a compelling critique of traditionally established practice but adds a broadened theoretical orientation that gives full recognition to the importance of cultural dynamics embedded in helping processes. The multicultural perspective emerges from a conception of culture as a "frame of reference" from which we encounter the world, ourselves, and life".

A variety of conceptualisations of "culturally competent" practice have been formulated in recent years in response to the failure of traditional practice theories to address multicultural diversities. Almost all of these models emphasize the need for practitioners to gain a profound understanding of the "worldview" or "cultural frame of reference" of the client. The most commonlyoffered approach to acquiring this kind of understanding has been what Dyche and Zayas call the *cultural literacy* approach. In this model, practitioners are encouraged to deepen their understanding of the client's life world by studying the history, backgrounds, and characteristic traits of diverse cultural groups.

Many practice textbooks follow this approach, presenting a wealth of culture-specific information and culture-specific practice recommendations organised under broad ethnic group categories, most commonly the four major American-designated ethnic groups of African Americans, Asian Americans, Native Americans, and Hispanic Americans.

Although the cultural literacy approach has served to draw attention to the centrality of culture in human experience, the model has several theoretical, conceptual, and practical weaknesses that limit its usefulness as a way of gaining an understanding of worldviews and cultural meanings.

First, the use of a group-membership conceptualisation of culture risks gross overgeneralisations while ignoring the extraordinary heterogeneity that exists within groups. It fails to recognise that people who share the same group membership often exhibit considerable cultural variation on a number of variables such as country of origin, generational status, socioeconomic status, education, preferred language, immigration history, in addition to the intersecting diversities of gender, age, sexual orientation, differential abilities, religious affiliation, and so on. Oftentimes normative, nomothetic information is difficult to distinguish from stereotypes, and may inadvertently elicit prejudice in the very attempt to avoid it.

Group-membership conceptualisations of culture are also problematic in that they divert attention from what Ho maintains is the more salient variable of "internalised culture," that is, the cultural elements internalised by persons from a variety of cultural systems. According to Ho, it is the client's internalised culture, not his or her cultural group membership, to which practitioners must attend. This model also places the practitioner in the powerful position of "expert knower" who needs to master information about other cultures in order to understand and work with people who are culturally "different". In these formulations, ethnicity tends to be framed as a client variable, rather than a characteristic of both practitioner and client..

A practical limitation is the impossibility of learning the cultural backgrounds of all the groups encountered in culturally diverse contexts. While the need for alternatives to the cultural literacy model have been widely noted, proponents of more phenomenologically or ethnographically oriented approaches have yet to offer a unifying conceptual framework, or to specifically address the issue of empathy in the context of diversity.

Ethnographic Perspective

No longer relegated to the study of cultures in far-off places, ethnography has "overflowed the banks of anthropology" and is increasingly recognised by a growing number of disciplines as offering a unique approach to understanding the meanings and intentions that shape the nature of human and social conduct. With its roots in symbolic interactionism and sociolinguistics, the essential core of ethnography is a concern with *meaning,* and one of the primary means for the investigation of meaning is ethnographic interviewing.

Though not always recognised, ethnography and social work espouse a surprisingly similar goal: to understand the human experience as it is lived, felt, and known by its participants. The usefulness of ethnographic methods to cross-cultural practice in the human services has been a primary theme in the work of Green and his associate Leigh. Their primary emphasis, however, has been on the way that practitioners can use informants, cultural guides, translators, indigenous healers, and field observations to "build a knowledge base" about a particular ethnic group—an emphasis akin to the cultural literacy approach. Green, for example, discusses how practitioners can gather cultural information from a number of clients until "a general picture of life in a given community" emerges. Similarly, Leigh suggests that the "accumulated data" from a number of interviews with clients can be used to "develop an agency profile of minority persons of color" or to construct "a classification of client conditions and possible treatments from a cultural perspective".

Clifford Geertz's interpretive ethnography is particularly illuminating in terms of the current discussion. Geertz is widely credited for revolutionising ethnography by advocating an interpretive analysis of culture "in search of meaning" rather than a scientific analysis "in search of laws". Geertz challenged the historic epistemological base of ethnography with its Cartesian assumptions of 'value free' inquiry and claims to 'objective' truth. Instead, he advocated for an emic or *verstehen* approach to understanding local knowledge and pluralist standpoints. For Geertz , the "whole point" of ethnographic inquiry is "to aid us in gaining access to the conceptual world in which our subjects live so that we can, in some extended sense of the term, converse with them". To commit oneself to an interpretive approach to the study of culture, he said, was to commit oneself to a view of ethnographic assertions as "essentially contestable". The practitioner can no longer presume to be able to present "an objective, noncontested account of the other's experience".

Geertz's ethnographic concepts of contextual meaning, local knowledge, pluralist standpoints, emic inquiry, contestable accounts, and interpretive understandings point the way to a broadened conceptualisation of empathy in the context of diversity. In particular, the following principles and processes are particularly salient.

Adopting the stance of learner. A critical feature of interpretive ethnography is the positioning of the professional, not as expert knower, but as learner. Ethnographers are trained to ask, "What do my informants know that I can discover?," as opposed to, "What expert knowledge do I posses which will help me explain this?". The ethnographic emphasis on the learner stance is strikingly similar to "not-knowing" stance of narrative therapists and the stance of naiveté and curiosity advocated by some multicultural scholars. Ethnographers say, in effect, "I am interested in finding out how you see things, how your talk about things. I want to understand things from your point of view".

By valuing and legitimating the knowledge and expertise of the other, the learner's stance encourages the expressions of multiple ideas and subjugated knowledges.

Listening for meaning. Although both ethnographers and practitioners place high value on attentive listening, ethnographic listening shifts the focus from listening for the "feelings" that underlie the client's words and actions, in favour of listening for underlying cultural "meanings". While multicultural practice theorists also emphasize the importance attending to cultural meanings, what ethnography adds to the discussion is its particular focus on "language" as a pathway to the discovery of meaning.

According to Spradley, "language is more than a means of communicating about reality: it is a tool for constructing reality". Language is not simply a tool for transmitting information; it estabiishes the meanings speakers assign to their experiences. In this regard, a key ethnographic concept is the "use principle", that is, rather than directly asking respondents, "What do you mean?," ethnographers attempt to discover *tacit* meanings by attending to the way that phrases and terms are used in ordinary language. Ethnographers are trained to be alert for "translation competence," that is, the tendency of people to "translate" their experience into a form which will be better understood by outsiders. The tendency to translate for outsiders is seen as distorting the cultural reality of the respondent.

Ethnographers instead attempt to elicit "untranslated" speech and meaning by repeatedly encouraging interviewees to tell their stories "in their own words". Ethnographers use strategies such as *restating* and *incorporating* key phrases and terms used by the respondent as a way of prioritising the respondents' voice over the professional's voice. These techniques stand in contrast to the traditional empathic techniques of *rephrasing* and *reframing*. The risk inherent in rephrasing, according to Green, is that professional language can override and distort client meanings.

Acknowledging power and sociopolitical context. The adoption of a learner's stance, and the prioritising of the client's voice, are both expressions of the ethnographic focus on reducing power differentials between inquirer and respondent. Ethnographers acknowledge that the interview itself takes place in a sociopolitical context of unequal power distributions based on race, class, gender and other socially constructed categories. In ethnographic research, respondents are often invited to participate as collaborators and co-researchers in the exploration of a given phenomenon.

Ethnography's acute attention to eliciting and documenting silenced and subjugated voices reflects its epistemological emphasis on a collaborative approach to understanding in which no one's perspectives are privileged. Ethnography's sensitivity to issues of dominance and power contrasts with the insufficient attention given to these issues in traditional empathy theory. Keefe is one of the few empathy theorists who emphasized the need for empathic attunement not only to "psychodynamics" but also to "dynamics of power and oppression."

Multicultural theorists, along with interpretive ethnographers, have been far more attentive than traditional empathy theorists to the ways in which experiences of entitlement and powerlessness shape perceptions, feelings, and behaviour. By incorporating multicultural and ethnographic perspectives into a discussion of empathy, the process of negotiating understanding broadens to include attunement to the sociopolitical context and power arrangements that shape human experience.

Negotiating understanding dialogically. In traditional conceptualisations of empathy, as well as in cultural literacy models, an understanding of the other's frame of reference depends largely on the clinical and cultural expertise of practitioners. In contrast, a key theoretical and practice concept in interpretive ethnography is that professionals initially abstain from interpretations based on preexisting frameworks. Theoretical preconceptions are held in abeyance in order to hear the client's story openly, without attempting to "make sense" of the story on the basis of practitioner assumptions.

Emerging understandings are framed as tentative hypotheses which are supported, disconfirmed, or modified by respondents themselves in a reciprocal, iterative exchange. Only at the end of the process do ethnographers look at how inductively-derived understandings fit with relevant theoretical materials.

The meaning of the experience is "named" through a collaborative, negotiated process. Although multicultural writers also emphasize collaborative processes, an important contribution of ethnography is the use of the "conversation" metaphor to underscore the mutual, dialogical nature of ethnographic knowing. Lambek concurs with Geertz that the goal of ethnographic inquiry is to create "a mutually comprehensible dialogue," and "a ground for further conversation".

In ethnography, "incommensurable discourses" are seen not as problematic but rather as "opening up a space" in which people can converse about the discordant elements of their experience. The gap or clash between various kinds meanings is what ultimately provides an ideal space for mutual learning. Conceptualisations of empathy can benefit from this concept that the "conversation" does not depend on shared meanings, only on shared *exploration* of meanings..

Engaging in Self-reflexivity. Although self-awareness of preconceived assumptions, values and biases is axiomatic in both traditional and multicultural theories of practice, ethnography moves beyond the rather passive notion of "self-awareness" and stresses the more active concept of "reflexivity." Vigilant and ongoing reflexivity is considered foundational to a recognition of the ways in which the autobiographies, cultures, and historical contexts of inquirers determine what they see and do not see. Reflexivity also differs in purpose from self-awareness. Multicultural scholars stress the need for practitioners to be "aware" of their biases and assumptions and to "ferret out" and eliminate private agendas, personal prejudices, and stereotypic perceptions of clients.

In ethnographic inquiry however, the control or elimination of bias is not assumed possible, nor even desirable. Subjectivity is not controlled but *incorporated* into the inquiry by making biases explicit and acknowledging how biases dictate questions and category construction. Ethnographers practice reflexivity through the writing of reflexive journals, field, notes, and memos. These writings contain the introspective record of ideas, fears, mistakes, confusion, breakthroughs and problems that arise in the course of inquiry. This emphasis on reflexivity is yet another conceptual contribution from ethnography to an enlarged conceptualisation of empathic processes.

A Conceptual Framework

The foregoing interdisciplinary analysis points to the need for a shift in the focus of empathy from the client's "self-experience" to the "lived experience", from the "internal" frame of reference to the "cultural" frame of reference. It is proposed that empathy be reconceptualised as a process of caring inquiry into the lived experience of the other, and a process of dialogically creating shared understanding of the cultural and contextual meanings that shape that experience. In short, empathy is both a mode of inquiry and a mode of bonding—a way of knowing, and a way of connection. The distinguishing features of a reconceptualisation of empathy are summarised below.

Traditional Empathy	*Reconceptualized Empathy*
client's reality	understanding seen as
seen as knowable	partial and fallible
attunement to underlying feelings	attunement to language and meaning
person-centered (cultural/sociopolitical)	context-centered
social locations ignored	social locations examined

expert stance	learner stance
practitioner understandings privileged	client understandings privileged
unidirectional	mutual and reciprocal
deductively-derived understanding	inductive, dialogical understanding
requires self-awareness	requires self-reflexivity

The proposed conceptual framework lays the ground for further research into the ways in which human beings come to know and understand one another in cross-cultural clinical practice. The framework proposed above is seen as provisional in that it is derived from an analysis and synthesis of theoretical literature. The next step is to engage in discovery-oriented research that probes the degree to which this theoretically-based conceptualisation of empathic processes "fits" with the lived experience of participants in cross-cultural clinical encounters. It is argued that future empathy research needs to be grounded in the lived experience of practitioners and clients in naturalistic settings, much as Rogers and Kohut formulated their ground-breaking theories from actual practice experience.

Interpretive methodologies would shift the primary focus of research from the identification of components of empathy to the "lived experience" of empathy and the processes by which participants in clinical encounters negotiate mutual understanding. Rather than viewing empathy as primarily a therapist behaviour, the focus shifts to the patterns of inquiry, dialogue, and reflection that promote or limit the coconstruction of understanding between dialogue partners.

Processes and patterns that are thought to be facilitative of empathic understanding could be systematically examined to see if they are associated with good engagement and other identified outcomes. Renewed research directed to illuminating the phenomenological nature and function of empathy is particularly important and timely in the current era of managed care in which the healing potential of relationships is being minimised over manualised approaches to practice. In the increasingly diverse and globalised context of social work practice, the capacity to empathise with other persons and perspectives—to negotiate mutual understanding and meaning—may well become one of the most important aspects of culturally competent practice.

Cultural Competence in Social Work

The social work profession traditionally has emphasized the importance of the person-in-environment and the dual perspective, the concept that all people are part of two systems: the larger societal system and their immediate environments. Social workers using a person-in-environment framework for assessment need to include to varying degrees important cultural factors that have meaning for clients and reflect the culture of the world around them.

In the United States, cultural diversity in social work has primarily been associated with race and ethnicity, but diversity is taking on a broader meaning to include the sociocultural experiences of people of different genders, social classes, religious and spiritual beliefs, sexual orientations, ages, and physical and mental abilities. These include addressing racial identity formation for people of color as well as for white people; the interrelationship among class, race, ethnicity, and gender; working with low-income families; working with older adults; the importance of religion and spirituality in the lives of clients; the development of gender identity and sexual orientation; immigration, acculturation, and assimilation stresses; biculturalism; working with people with disabilities; empowerment skills; community building; reaching out to new populations of color; and how to train for culturally competent models of practice.

Therefore, cultural competence in social work practice implies a heightened consciousness of how clients experience their uniqueness and deal with their differences and similarities within a larger social context.

Cultural competence refers to the process by which individuals and systems respond respectfully and effectively to people of all cultures, languages, classes, races, ethnic backgrounds, religions, and other diversity factors in a manner that recognises, affirms, and values the worth of individuals, families, and communities and protects and preserves the dignity of each.

"Cultural competence is a set of congruent behaviors, attitudes, and policies that come together in a system or agency or among professionals and enable the system, agency, or professionals to work effectively in cross-cultural situations".

Operationally defined, cultural competence is the integration and transformation of knowledge about individuals and groups of people into specific standards, policies, practices, and attitudes used in appropriate cultural settings to increase the quality of services, thereby producing better outcomes. Competence in cross-cultural functioning means learning new patterns of behavior and effectively applying them in appropriate settings.

Gallegos provided one of the first conceptualisations of ethnic competence as "a set of procedures and activities to be used in acquiring culturally relevant insights into the problems of minority clients and the means of applying such insights to the development of intervention strategies that are culturally appropriate for these clients." This kind of sophisticated cultural competence does not come naturally to any social worker and requires a high level of professionalism and knowledge.

There are five essential elements that contribute to a system's ability to become more culturally competent. The system should (1) value diversity, (2) have the capacity for cultural self-assessment, (3) be conscious of the dynamics inherent when cultures interact, (4) institutionalise cultural knowledge, and (5) develop programs and services that reflect an understanding of diversity between and within cultures. These five elements must be manifested in every level of the service delivery system. They should be reflected in attitudes, structures, policies, and services.

Cultural Competence and Social Diversity

- Social workers should understand culture and its functions in human behavior and society, recognising the strengths that exist in all cultures.
- Social workers should have a knowledge base of their clients' cultures and be able to demonstrate competence in the provision of services that are sensitive to clients' cultures and to differences among people and cultural groups.
- Social workers should obtain education about and seek to understand the nature of social diversity and oppression with respect to race, ethnicity, national origin, color, sex, sexual orientation, age, marital status, political belief, religion, and mental or physical disability.

Social and Political Action

Social workers should act to expand choice and opportunity for all people, with special regard for vulnerable, disadvantaged, oppressed, and exploited people and groups.

Social workers should promote conditions that encourage respect for cultural and social diversity within the United States and globally. Social workers should promote policies and practices that demonstrate respect for difference, support the expansion of cultural knowledge and resources, advocate for programs and institutions that demonstrate cultural competence, and promote policies that safeguard the rights of and confirm equity and social justice for all people. Social workers should act to prevent and eliminate domination of, exploitation of, and discrimination against any person, group, or class on the basis of race, ethnicity, national origin, color, sex, sexual orientation, age, marital status, political belief, religion, or mental or physical disability.

Goals and Objectives of the Standards

These standards address the need for definition, support, and encouragement for the development of a high level of social work practice that encourages cultural competence among all social workers so that they can respond effectively, knowledgeably, sensitively, and skillfully to the diversity inherent in the agencies in which they work and with the clients and communities they serve.

The specific goals of the standards are

- to maintain and improve the quality of culturally competent services provided by social workers and programs delivered by social service agencies
- to establish professional expectations so that social workers can monitor and evaluate their culturally competent practice
- to provide a framework for social workers to assess culturally competent practice

- to inform consumers, governmental regulatory bodies, and others, such as insurance carriers, about the profession's standards for culturally competent practice
- to establish specific ethical guidelines for culturally competent social work practice in agency or private practice settings
- to provide documentation of professional expectations for agencies, peer review committees, state regulatory bodies, insurance carriers, and others.

Standards for Cultural Competence in Social Work Practice

Standard 1. Ethics and Values

Social workers shall function in accordance with the values, ethics, and standards of the profession, recognising how personal and professional values may conflict with or accommodate the needs of diverse clients.

A major characteristic of a profession is its ability to establish ethical standards to help professionals identify ethical issues in practice and to guide them in determining what is ethically acceptable and unacceptable behavior. There are several key elements in social work practice, mainly the social workers' commitment to enhancing human well-being and helping meet basic human needs of all people; client empowerment; service to people who are vulnerable and oppressed; focus on individual well-being in a social context; promotion of social justice and social change; and sensitivity to cultural and ethnic diversity. Social workers clearly have an ethical responsibility to be culturally competent practitioners.

Accepted practice in one culture may be prohibited in another. To fully understand and appreciate these differences, social workers must be familiar with varying cultural traditions and norms. Clients' cultural backgrounds may affect their help-seeking behaviors as well. The ways in which social services are planned and implemented need to be culturally sensitive to be culturally effective. Cultural competence builds on the profession's valued stance on self-determination and individual dignity and worth, adding inclusion, tolerance, and respect for diversity in all its forms. It requires social workers to struggle with ethical dilemmas arising from value conflicts or special needs of diverse clients such as helping clients enroll in mandated training or mental health services that are culturally insensitive.

Cultural competence requires social workers to recognise the strengths that exist in all cultures. This does not imply a universal nor automatic acceptance of all practices of all cultures. For example, some cultures subjugate women, oppress persons based on sexual orientation, and value the use of corporal punishment and the death penalty.

Standard 2. Self-Awareness

Social workers shall develop an understanding of their own personal and cultural values and beliefs as a first step in appreciating the importance of multicultural identities in the lives of people.

Cultural competence requires social workers to examine their own cultural backgrounds and identities to increase awareness of personal assumptions, values, and biases. The workers' self-awareness of their own cultural identities is as fundamental to practice as the informed assumptions about clients' cultural backgrounds and experiences in the United States. This awareness of personal values, beliefs, and biases inform their practice and influence relationships with clients. Cultural competence includes knowing and acknowledging how fears, ignorance, and the "isms" (racism, sexism, ethnocentrism, heterosexism, ageism, classism) have influenced their attitudes, beliefs, and feelings.

Social workers need to be able to move from being culturally aware of their own heritage to becoming culturally aware of the heritage of others. They can value and celebrate differences in others rather than maintain an ethnocentric stance and can demonstrate comfort with differences between themselves and others. They have an awareness of personal and professional limitations that may warrant the referral of a client to another social worker or agency that can best meet the clients' needs. Self-awareness also helps in understanding the process of cultural identity formation and helps guard against stereotyping. As one develops the diversity within one's own group, one can be more open to the diversity within other groups.

Cultural competence also requires social workers to appreciate how workers need to move from cultural awareness to cultural sensitivity before achieving cultural competence and to evaluate growth and development throughout these different levels of cultural competence in practice.

Self-awareness becomes the basis for professional development and should be supported by supervision and agency administration. Agency administrators and public policy advocates also need to develop strategies to reduce their own biases and expand their self-awareness.

Standard 3. Cross-Cultural Knowledge

Social workers shall have and continue to develop specialised knowledge and understanding about the history, traditions, values, family systems, and artistic expressions of major client groups served.

Cultural competence is not static and requires frequent relearning and unlearning about diversity.

Social workers need to take every opportunity to expand their cultural knowledge and expertise by expanding their understanding of the following areas: "the impact of culture on behavior, attitudes, and values; the help-seeking behaviors of diverse client groups; the role of language, speech patterns, and communication styles of various client groups in the communities served; the impact of social service policies on various client groups; the resources (agencies, people, informal helping networks, and research) that can be used on behalf of diverse client groups; the ways that professional values may conflict with or accommodate the needs of diverse client groups; and the power relationships in the community, agencies, or institutions and their impact on diverse client groups".

Social workers need to possess specific knowledge about the particular providers and client groups they work with, including the range of historical experiences, resettlement patterns, individual and group oppression, adjustment styles, socioeconomic backgrounds, life processes, learning styles, cognitive skills, worldviews and specific cultural customs and practices, their definition of and beliefs about the causation of wellness and illness or normality and abnormality, and how care and services should be delivered.

Cultural competence requires explicit knowledge of traditional theories and principles concerning such areas as human behavior, life cycle development, problem-solving skills, prevention, and rehabilitation. Social workers need the critical skill of asking the right questions, being comfortable with discussing cultural differences, and asking clients about what works for them and what is comfortable for them in these discussions. Furthermore, culturally competent social workers need to know the limitations and strengths of current theories, processes and practice models, and which have specific applicability and relevance to the service needs of culturally diverse client groups.

Standard 4. Cross-Cultural Skills

Social workers shall use appropriate methodological approaches, skills, and techniques that reflect the workers' understanding of the role of culture in the helping process.

The personal attributes of a culturally competent social worker include qualities that reflect genuineness, empathy, and warmth; the capacity to respond flexibly to a range of possible solutions; an acceptance of and openness to differences among people; a willingness to learn to work with clients of different backgrounds; an articulation and clarification of stereotypes and biases and how these may accommodate or conflict with the needs of diverse client groups; and personal commitment to alleviate racism, sexism, homophobia, ageism, and poverty. These attributes are important to the direct practitioner and to the agency administrator.

More specifically, social workers should have the skills to

- work with a wide range of people who are culturally different or similar to themselves, and establish avenues for learning about the cultures of these clients
- assess the meaning of culture for individual clients and client groups, encourage open discussion of differences, and respond to culturally biased cues
- master interviewing techniques that reflect an understanding of the role of language in the client's culture
- conduct a comprehensive assessment of client systems in which cultural norms and behaviors are

evaluated as strengths and differentiated from problematic or symptomatic behaviors

- integrate the information gained from a culturally competent assessment into culturally appropriate intervention plans and involve clients and respect their choices in developing goals for service
- select and develop appropriate methods, skills, and techniques that are attuned to their clients' cultural, bicultural, or marginal experiences in their environments
- generate a wide variety of verbal and nonverbal communication skills in response to direct and indirect communication styles of diverse clients
- understand the interaction of the cultural systems of the social worker, the client, the particular agency setting, and the broader immediate community
- effectively use the clients' natural support system in resolving problems—for example, folk healers, storefronts, religious and spiritual leaders, families of creation, and other community resources
- demonstrate advocacy and empowerment skills in work with clients, recognising and combating the "isms", stereotypes, and myths held by individuals and institutions
- identify service delivery systems or models that are appropriate to the targeted client population and make appropriate referrals when indicated
- consult with supervisors and colleagues for feedback and monitoring of performance and identify features of their own professional style that impede or enhance their culturally competent practice
- evaluate the validity and applicability of new techniques, research, and knowledge for work with diverse client groups.

Standard 5. Service Delivery

Social workers shall be knowledgeable about and skillful in the use of services available in the community and broader society and be able to make appropriate referrals for their diverse clients.

Agencies and professional social work organisations need to promote cultural competence by supporting the evaluation of culturally competent service delivery models and setting standards for cultural competence within these settings. Culturally competent social workers need to be aware of and vigilant about the dynamics that result from cultural differences and similarities between workers and clients. This includes monitoring cultural competence among social workers (agency evaluations, supervision, in-service training, and feedback from clients).

Social workers need to detect and prevent exclusion of diverse clients from service opportunities and seek to create opportunities for clients, matching their needs with culturally competent service delivery systems or adapting services to better meet the culturally unique needs of clients. Furthermore, they need to foster policies and procedures that help ensure access to care that accommodates varying cultural beliefs. For direct practitioners, policymakers, or administrators, this specifically involves

- actively recruiting multiethnic staff and including cultural competence requirements in job descriptions and performance and promotion measures
- reviewing the current and emergent demographic trends for the geographic area served by the agency to determine service needs for the provision of interpretation and translation services

- creating service delivery systems or models that are more appropriate to the targeted client populations or advocating for the creation of such services
- including participation by clients as major stakeholders in the development of service delivery systems
- ensuring that program decor and design is reflective of the cultural heritage of clients and families using the service
- attending to social issues (for example, housing, education, police, and social justice) that concern clients of diverse backgrounds
- not accepting staff remarks that insult or demean clients and their culture
- supporting the inclusion of cultural competence standards in accreditation bodies and organisational policies as well as in licensing and certification examinations
- developing staffing plans that reflect the organisation and the targeted client population (for example, hiring, position descriptions, performance evaluations, training)
- developing performance measures to assess culturally competent practice
- including participation of client groups in the development of research and treatment protocols.

Standard 6. Empowerment and Advocacy

Social workers shall be aware of the effect of social policies and programs on diverse client populations, advocating for and with clients whenever appropriate.

Culturally competent social workers are keenly aware of the deleterious effects of racism, sexism, ageism, heterosexism or homophobia, anti-Semitism, ethnocentrism, classism, and xenophobia on clients' lives and the need for social advocacy and social action to better empower diverse clients and communities. As first defined by Solomon, empowerment involves facilitating the clients' connection with their own power and, in turn, being empowered by the very act of reaching across cultural barriers. Empowerment refers to the person's ability to do for themselves while advocacy implies doing for the client. Even in the act of advocacy, social workers must be careful not to impose their values on clients and must seek to understand what clients mean by advocacy. Respectful collaboration needs to take place to promote mutually agreed-on goals for change.

Social workers need a range of skills and abilities to advocate for and with clients against the underlying devaluation of cultural experiences related to difference and oppression and power and privilege in the United States. The empowerment tradition in social work practice suggests a promotion of the combined goals of consciousness raising and developing a sense of personal power and skills while working toward social change. Best practice views this as a process and outcome of the empowerment perspective. Social workers using this standard will apply an ecosystems perspective and a strengths orientation in practice. This means that workers consider client situations as they describe needs in terms of transitory challenges rather than fixed problems. According to Gutiérrez and Lewis, empowerment is a model for practice, a perspective and a set of skills and techniques. The expectation is that culturally competent social workers reflect these values in their practice.

Standard 7. Diverse Workforce

Social workers shall support and advocate for recruitment, admissions and hiring, and retention efforts in social work programs and agencies that ensure diversity within the profession.

Increasing cultural competence within the profession requires demonstrated efforts to recruit and retain a diverse cadre of social workers, many of whom would bring some "indigenous" cultural competence to the profession as well as demonstrated efforts to increase avenues for the acquisition of culturally competent skills by all social workers. Diversity should be represented at all levels of the organisation, and not just among direct practitioners.

The social work profession has espoused a commitment to diversity, inclusion, and affirmative action. However, available statistics indicate that in the United States social workers are predominantly white (88.5 percent) and female (78.0 percent). The proportion of people of color has remained relatively stable in the social work membership of the National Association of Social Workers over a period of several years: 5.3 percent identify themselves as African American; Hispanics, including Mexican Americans, Puerto Ricans, and other Hispanic groups constitute about 2.8 percent of the membership; Asians and Pacific Islanders 1.7 percent; and American Indians/First Nations People 0.5 percent. Social work client populations are more diverse than the social work profession itself. In many instances, service to clients is targeted to marginalised communities and special populations, groups that typically include disproportionately high numbers of people of color, elderly people, people with disabilities, and clients of lower socioeconomic status.

Matching workforce to client populations can be an effective strategy for bridging cultural differences between social worker and client, although it cannot be the only strategy. The assumption is that individuals of similar backgrounds can understand each other better and communicate more effectively. Yet an equally compelling fact is that "the majority of clinicians from the mainstream dominant culture will routinely provide care for large numbers of patients of diverse ethnic and/or cultural backgrounds. Clearly increasing the numbers of culturally diverse social workers is not sufficient. Even these professionals will need to be able to provide care for patients who are not like themselves". In addition, culturally competent social workers who bring a special skill or knowledge to the profession, like bicultural and bilingual skills, or American Sign Language (ASL) skills, are entitled to professional equity and should not be exploited for their expertise but should be appropriately compensated for skills that enhance the delivery of services to clients.

Standard 8. Professional Education

Social workers shall advocate for and participate in educational and training programs that help advance cultural competence within the profession.

Cultural competence is a vital link between the theoretical and practice knowledge base that defines social work expertise. Social work is a practice-oriented profession, and social work education and training need to keep up with and stay ahead of changes in professional practice, which includes the changing needs of diverse client populations. Diversity needs to be addressed in social work curricula and needs to be viewed as central to faculty and staff appointments and research agendas.

The social work profession should be encouraged to take steps to ensure cultural competence as an integral part of social work education, training and practice, and to increase research and scholarship on culturally competent practice among social work professionals. This includes undergraduate, master's and doctoral programs in social work as well as post-master's training, continuing education, and meetings of the profession. Social agencies should be encouraged to provide culturally competent in-service training and opportunities for continuing education for agency-based workers.

Standard 9. Language Diversity

Social workers shall seek to provide and advocate for the provision of information, referrals, and services in the language appropriate to the client, which may include the use of interpreters.

Social workers should accept the individual person in his or her totality and ensure access to needed services. Language is a source and an extension of personal identity and culture and therefore, is one way individuals interact with others in their families and communities and across different cultural groups. Individuals and groups have a right to use their language in their individual and communal life.

Language diversity is a resource for society, and linguistic diversity should be preserved and promoted. The essence of the social work profession is to promote social justice and eliminate discrimination and oppression based on linguistic or other diversities. Agencies and providers of services are expected to take reasonable steps to provide services and information in appropriate language other than English to ensure that people with limited English proficiency are effectively informed and can effectively participate in and benefit from its programs.

It is the responsibility of social services agencies and social workers to provide clients services in the language of their choice or to seek the assistance of qualified language interpreters. Social workers need to communicate respectfully and effectively with clients from different ethnic, cultural, and linguistic backgrounds; this might include knowing the client's language. The use of language translation should be done by trained professional interpreters (for example, certified or registered sign language interpreters). Interpreters generally need proficiency in both English and the other language, as well as orientation and training.

Social agencies and social workers have a responsibility to use language interpreters when necessary, and to make certain that interpreters do not breach confidentiality, create barriers to clients when revealing personal information that is critical to their situation, are properly trained and oriented to the ethics of interpreting in a helping situation, and have fundamental knowledge of specialised terms and concepts specific to the agency's programs or activities.

Standard 10. Cross-Cultural Leadership

Social workers shall be able to communicate information about diverse client groups to other professionals.

Social work is the appropriate profession to take a leadership role not only in disseminating knowledge about diverse client groups, but also in actively advocating for fair and equitable treatment of all clients served. This role should extend within and outside the profession. Diversity skills, defined as sensitivity to diversity, multicultural leadership, acceptance and tolerance, cultural competence, and tolerance of ambiguity, constitute one of the core leadership skills for successful leadership.

Social workers should come forth to assume leadership in empowering diverse client populations, to share information about diverse populations to the general public, and to advocate for their clients' concerns at interpersonal and institutional levels, locally, nationally, and internationally. With the establishment of standards for cultural competence in social work practice, there is an equally important need for the profession to provide ongoing training in cultural competence and to establish mechanisms for the evaluation of competence-based practice. As the social work profession develops cultural competencies, then the profession must have the ability to measure those competencies. The development of outcome measures needs to go hand in hand with the development of these standards.

13

Social Work Organisations

Social workers were active in important international movements of the early 20th century, especially movements for peace, women's rights, and improved labour conditions. As leaders in social welfare from various countries met each other, the benefits of exchanges of ideas became evident. This led to a proposal for an international conference on social work and social welfare, an idea that originated when European and Japanese social workers participated in the U.S. National Conference of Social Work in 1919.

The official proposal for a conference was made in a letter from Dr. Rene Sand of Belgium to Julia Lathrop of the U.S. in 1923. Endorsement by national associations and by the League of Red Cross Societies followed. In 1926, an organising committee met in Paris; the Committee was comprised of representatives from 17 countries in Europe, Asia and North America and from a number of important international organisations. Among these were the League of Nations, the International Labour Organisation, the League of Red Cross Societies, the International Migration Service, and the Save the Children Fund.

Leading the way were Dr. Alice Masarykova of Prague as President and Dr. Rene Sand as Secretary

General of the conference. Plans grew until the final event spanned two weeks and included international meetings of a number of organisations. The first International Conference of Social Work was held from July 8-13 1928 in Paris and was attended by 2,481 delegates from 42 countries. It is remarkable that so many travelled great distances almost 80 years ago.

The Conference was only the first of what became the international social work and social welfare conferences. Two more were held before World War II interrupted international collaboration: 1932 in Frankfurt and 1936 in London. A planned conference for 1940 was never held; a planning meeting in Paris in 1946 and much less grandiose conference in 1948 in Atlantic City, New Jersey in the U.S. began the effort to rebuild the international social work/social welfare movement.

Although they have been slightly renamed, both the IASSW and the ICSW have been in continuous existence since the 1928 meeting. The IFSW, originally the International Permanent Secretariat of Social Workers, disappeared for a time, but was officially reconstituted in 1956, as will be described below.

International Federation of Social Workers (IFSW)

The International Federation of Social Workers (IFSW) is a global organisation striving for social justice, human rights and social development through the development of social work, best practices and international cooperation between social workers and their professional organisations. Association members work together through the international organisation towards developing the common goals of the profession and in working on issues of concern to social workers globally. IFSW tries to achieve this international identity by:

- encouraging co-operation between social workers of all countries;
- providing means for discussion and the exchange of ideas and experience through meetings, study visits, research projects, exchanges, publications and other methods of communication;
- establishing and maintaining relationships with social work organisations and their members and representing them to international bodies relevant to social development and welfare;
- sponsoring biennial international symposia and conferences;
- developing and publishing policy statements to guide social work practice worldwide;
- advocating for the protection of human rights of practicing social workers; and
- providing consultation to the United Nations on issues of human development and human rights.

The IFSW celebrated its 50th jubilee in Munich in 2006, having grown from just 12 member organisations in 1956, to over 80 today. However, as noted above, the heritage of the modern IFSW stretches back to the First International Conference on Social Work held in Paris in July 1928, where it was agreed that an international association of social workers be formed.

At the 1932 Second International Conference on Social Work held in Frankfurt, provisional statutes of the International Permanent Secretariat of Social Workers (IPSSW) were agreed. The IPSSW operated from Berlin, Geneva and Prague until 1956 when the International Federation of Social Workers was formed in Munich with 12 national member organisations and a new Secretariat was established in New York, sharing office with the National Association of Social Workers.

Of major concern to the new organisation was the question of ethics and in 1957 work began on the establishment of what has become today 'Ethics of Social Work - Statement of Principles'. The President and Executive promoted the voice of social work at the United Nations and its bodies so much that by 1959, just three years after re-establishment, the IFSW was approved for consultative status with the United Nations Economic and Social Council (ECOSOC), with a special relationship later extended by UNICEF and the International Labour Organisation (ILO).

Teams of representatives are in action at the United Nations in Geneva, Nairobi, New York and Vienna. IFSW now also has formal partnerships with Amnesty International, CONGO (Conference of Non-Governmental Organisations in Consultative Relationship with the UN), Council of Europe; European Union, Habitat, IASSW and ICSW. Encouraging a discourse of international social work was greatly strengthened by the decision to launch the Journal of International Social Work. IFSW joined its partner organisations, ICSW and IASSW in sponsoring the journal in 1959.

The Journal remains one of the most significant refereed journals on international social work available today. While early conferences were held jointly, by the mid 1960's it became apparent that for various reasons the three foundation organisations, IFSW, IASSW and ICSW, had begun to move in their own directions; since then, some of the conferences have been held separately and some together. Regional IFSW seminars and conferences have been a strong feature, particularly of the European region, and have extended with differing levels of success across all IFSW regions.

The IFSW Executive Committee decided to establish a permanent and paid secretariat in 1972 in Basel, Switzerland, appointing Catherine Chuard, followed by

Andrew Mouravieff-Apostol as the Secretary General, assisted in his work by his wife Ellen. Both enjoyed extensive networks within the United Nations system and Ellen remains today as the IFSW Main Representative to the UN Geneva. From 1975 to 1992 Andy was IFSW Secretary General, and was elected lifelong Honorary President when he retired in 1992.

For IFSW, Andy was the cornerstone. He communicated with social workers of all countries with warmth, knowledge and diplomacy and became like a father for the international social work community. His lifetime spanned close to a century and his history and background reflect the international character of the profession. Born in France in 1913 of Russian/Ukrainian parents, his family were abroad when the 1917 revolution in Russia broke out it was impossible for the aristocratic family to return home; Andy was only able to return to Russia at the time of perestroika in the late 1980s.

Working first as a journalist and then as a foreign correspondent in England before and during World War II, he also served in the Free French military forces. After the war Andy left journalism and took up a position with the World Council of Churches and later with the United Nations High Commissioner for Refugees. He served in many countries, but mainly in South America, where he met his future wife Ellen. The couple settled in Geneva, where Andy until his death worked as a professional interpreter at the United Nations and other international bodies.

The strengthening of the secretariat also heralded an era of increased activity in membership levels and by IFSW through its representative status with various organisations. The secretariat later moved to Oslo, Norway in 1992 and then in 1999 to Berne, Switzerland, where it is located today, with Tom Johannesen as the Secretary-General. The late 1970's saw considerable work undertaken on the definition of social work. This document was endorsed at the Brighton Conference in 1982 and remained unaltered until 1996 when a committee was established to revise and prepare a new definition of social work, ultimately adopted by both practitioners and educators in 2001.

The 1980's were particularly active years for the IFSW in the area of human rights and social justice. By this time the IFSW had well established representative teams to the United Nations in New York, Geneva and Vienna. This focus of concern led the Federation to a strong engagement in the UN International Year of Peace 1986, recognised by the UN officially declaring IFSW a 'Peace Messenger'. Eight years later the United Nations designated IFSW as 'Patron of the International Year of the Family' for exemplary support of the UN programme.

Many outstanding social workers have contributed over the years to IFSW and its development. Among these are Jane Hoey whose major contribution to social work was in the establishment and enforcement of standards in public welfare administration in the United States, and in whose name a fund has been established to promote social work in developing regions of the world. Another is Chauncey Alexander who served as the first US President of IFSW 1980-1982, developing the concept of global policy papers, the international code of ethics, and mentoring and promoting other social work associations.

Social work grew out of humanitarian and democratic ideals, and its values are based on respect for the equality, worth, and dignity of all people. Human rights and social justice serve as the motivation and justification for social work action. IFSW promotes human rights by publishing statements on human rights issues and related matters and by raising awareness within the profession about the profession's commitment to its human rights heritage. IFSW has adopted an International Policy on Human Rights describing its commitment and giving guidance to social workers and social work organisations on human rights policy matters.

To implement the human rights agenda of IFSW a special commission has been set up—the Human Rights Commission. Apart from its work on behalf of imprisoned and persecuted social workers around the world, the Commission has successfully developed two landmark publications with international partners, on human rights and social work and social work and the rights of the child. IFSW and its member Associations have also produced other academic publications from time to time.

Social Work and Globalisation was produced as a special issue on the occasion of the IFSW and IASSW joint Conference in Montreal, 2000. Other publications include a series of edited books on social work in different countries, Social Work Around the World, which is now on its fourth issue. Regional newsletters and journals are also published wherever possible.

A series of international policy papers has been developed and are regularly revised. Current policy papers cover Displaced Persons, Globalisation and the Environment, Health, HIV/AIDS, Indigenous Peoples, Women, Migration, Older Persons, Peace and Social Justice, Protection of Personal Information, Conditions in Rural Communities, Refugees and Youth.

A highlight in the 1990's was IFSW's strong involvement in the World Summit for Social Development in Copenhagen in 1995. A special issue of the IFSW Newsletter was presented to a broader audience focusing on social work contributions to a new world order for social development in the areas of poverty eradication, unemployment, social integration and transition in Eastern Europe. Also the Fourth UN World Conference on Women in Beijing the same year had a strong IFSW presence.

The start of the new century brought with it a significant range of challenges for the social work professions. A worldwide shift in political orientation towards conservative and in some instances ultra-conservative governments has meant that working to develop social services has been particularly difficult in more developed countries.

Issues concerning the alleviation of poverty, human rights and HIV/AIDS continue to be major concerns. IFSW has responded to some of the major international issues experiences in recent years such as the Asian tsunami, serious human rights violations in the Sudan and the challenges faced by orphans and vulnerable children in Africa, through projects initiated by its regional bodies and in cooperation with partner organisations.

IFSW is the international organisation representing professional social workers, although membership is through national social work organisations, not individual status. Only one national professional organisation in each country may become a member of the Federation. Such an organisation may be a national organisation or a coordinating body representing two or more national organisations. Each member association or coordinating body must observe the IFSW Constitution and should require from its members regular professional training based upon an organised sequence of social work education incorporating ethical standards of practice and a body of knowledge compatible with social work principles.

At present, there are national organisations in 84 countries in membership, representing just under 500,000 social workers across the world. Association members collaborate together through IFSW towards developing the common goals of the profession and in working on issues of concern to social workers internationally. IFSW is divided into the five geographical regions of Africa; Asia-Pacific; Europe; Latin America and the Caribbean; and North America, each of which is represented by a regional president.

An international elected executive committee steers the work of the Federation with a global President and Secretary General heading the body. The general executive meets every two years at the same time as an international Conference, at times held jointly with IASSW and ICSW. IFSW also has a very successful programme called 'Friends of IFSW,' providing affiliating social workers, social work students and organisations a link to international social work.

IFSW has faced significant challenges at various times in its history, often due to political and ideological differences among its many members. However the international executive committee and the General Meeting of the member associations has made every effort to work in as harmonious a way as possible and to reconcile and overcome these issues. Serious problems have ranged from conflicts in places as varied as the Middle East, Sri Lanka and Zimbabwe. However the contentious issue of South Africa was one of the most significant, when by 1963 the attention of the world began to focus on South Africa and its Apartheid policy.

The South African European Social Workers organisation was a member of IFSW at that time and despite continued work on their part to establish a coordinating body of European and non-European social workers, due to government policies in that country, such an organisation could not be established.

The principles of non-discrimination are foundation principles for social work and after many years of agonised debate and attempts to resolve this very difficult and 'delicate situation South Africa was expelled from membership in 1970 and was not eligible to re-enter membership again until 1998. In fact, South Africa has yet to achieve membership of IFSW due to the persistent problem of being able to form a coordinating body between the white, coloured and black South African social work associations.

There are various future priorities and challenges that face IFSW, including:

– A core concern is to ensure that key policy statements are up-to-date and relevant. In this context both IFSW and IASSW have agreed a four-year process for the review of the international definition of social work and the international statement of ethical principles, leading to the 2010 joint conference in Hong Kong. Thereafter these core statements will be reviewed every 10 years.

– Social work practice is becoming increasingly international with the migration of social workers from many countries in the developing world to the developed. A challenge for IFSW is to link with other organisations that are trying to improve conditions in the originating countries and stem this migration as far as this is possible.

– Conflicts and consequent human rights abuses have intensified throughout many regions of the world in recent years and this challenges IFSW to take an even higher profile in defence of human rights. IFSW already issues statements of concern where violations of peoples' rights occurs, such as in

Darfur, but the challenge for IFSW is to ensure that these words are translated into actions.

- A similar challenge for IFSW is to respond as effectively as it can to natural disasters such as the Asian tsunami of December 2004.
- The IFSW's engagement with debates on poverty, ways to achieve the Millennium Development Goals and tackle the consequences of HIV/AIDS remain important areas of concern for the organisation.

An enormous commitment by many volunteers and a small but dedicated secretariat has over 50 years given rise to a significant organisation with good reason to celebrate its achievements. Through a number of world and regional conferences, the development of core international documents to guide social work concepts and practices, and ongoing representation at the United Nations and other international bodies, IFSW is today a key global voice of international social work practice.

International Association of Schools of Social Work

The International Association of Schools of Social Work is the main organisation representing social work education and educators around the world; in 2008, it will celebrate its 80th anniversary.

The primary mission of the IASSW is to strengthen social work education around the world. This has remained constant since the founding. The most recent formal review of the mission statement took place in 2000 and resulted in the following mission statement:

"The International Association of Schools of Social Work is an international association of institutions of social work education, organisations supporting social work education and social work educators. Its mission is:

— To develop and promote excellence in social work education, research and scholarship globally in order to enhance human well-being;
— To create and maintain a dynamic community of social work educators and their programmes;
— To support and facilitate participation in mutual exchanges of information and expertise;
— To represent social work education at the international level."

The statement also commits IASSW to adhere to UN human rights declarations and conventions and to pursue social justice and social development.

A special section of the 1928 conference focused on social work education and was led by Alice Salomon of Germany. The delegates at the conference decided to "write to all the training schools of social work asking them whether they would be prepared to become members of an International Association of Schools". In addition to Alice Salomon, the founders of the International Committee of Schools of Social Work, as it was originally called, consisted of representatives from the Netherlands, Belgium, and Switzerland, soon joined by the United States, France, England, and Poland.

Of the 111 schools of social work identified at the time, 46 schools from 10 countries agreed to become founding members of the new association. By 1939, membership had grown to 75 schools from 18 countries; by then, however, all German schools had withdrawn from membership. In the early years, the International Committee sponsored seminars to exchange knowledge and strengthen social work education, including "summer schools"-seminars that intensively explored significant topics for social work.

The organisation continued to be led by Alice Salomon as President. She was pressured by her colleagues in Germany to resign after the Nazis came to power; Salomon was suspect for many reasons, including Jewish ancestry and her commitment to peace and internationalism. She resigned several times as President, but each time, her IASSW colleagues renamed her President. Just before she was expelled from Germany, Salomon completed the first world survey of social work education, published by the ICSSW in 1937. She produced an in-depth sociological and comparative analysis of social work education in 32 countries.

The International Committee established working relationships with the ILO and with the Commission on Social Questions of the League of Nations. A particularly important achievement was that the ILO set up a Centre of Documentation for schools of social work in 1929. "For the next ten years the ILO attempted, with moderate success, to collect and index the statutes, programmes of study, annual reports, publications, research and seminar reports, and lists of theses or other student reports from more than 100 schools of social work".

As was true for each of the 3 organisations, World War II had a devastating effect. Not only were communications disrupted for the war period, but many teachers and students died and educational facilities destroyed. The plight of the school at Warsaw is recorded in early letters of the IASSW:

> "I appeal most warmly in the name of the Board...to make their members send all they possibly can collect, books, papers, reports, etc. regarding social work to Mrs. Helena Radlinska, one of the founders of our Committee, professor of the State University of Lodz (Poland). Mrs. Radlinska had the great misfortune to see destroyed besides her private house, the School of Social Work, founded by her at the University of Warsaw as well as the University itself, and to lose by death two-thirds of the

> teaching staff. In spite of this great misfortune starting anew at the age of 75 years Mrs. Radlinska does what she can to rebuild a School of Social Work at the University of Lodz".

Kendall labelled the years 1945-1954 the "Restoration Years". A small conference was held in Atlantic City in the U.S. in 1948 and Rene Sand had agreed in 1946 to take on the Presidency of the International Committee of Schools of Social Work. Ironically, although devastation was significant, Kendall reports that the war and its aftermath created a new demand for social workers and thus, "by 1948, 359 schools were counted in 41 countries" in a report issued by the new United Nations.. Social work as a profession and social work educational institutions began to disappear in the Communist countries, but grew substantially in the newly independent countries in Asia and Africa.

In the 1950's and 1960's, IASSW extended its outreach to programmes in developing countries. The Congress was held in Madras, India in 1952, marking the first time the conference was held outside of Europe or North America. By 1956, the board of directors included members from Australia, Guatemala, Japan and India. The name of the organisation was officially changed to the International Association of Schools of Social Work, although many member units are not independent schools but programmes within larger institutions. A major, but sadly temporary, milestone was the establishment of a Secretariat in 1971 with a paid Secretary General.

Katherine Kendall served as the first paid Secretary General from 1971-1978. Originally in New York, the Secretariat moved to Vienna in 1978. Kendall was succeeded by Margarite Mathieu of Canada and then Vera Mehta of India. In the early 1990's, the organisation experienced financial difficulties caused by the increased expenses of maintaining the Vienna office. A decision was taken by the Board to return to a volunteer-run organisation and the Secretariat was closed in 1992. While finances have since permitted the hiring of an Administrative Assistant based in the office of the President, from 1993 IASSW has functioned without a professional executive officer.

As is true for ICSW and IFSW, IASSW holds a biennial world conference. These have been held regularly since 1928 except for the war years. At various times, the conferences have been held jointly with IFSW or with both IFSW and ICSW; in 2006 and 2008, the 3 organisations held/will hold separate conferences before joining in 3-way collaboration in 2010. It might be argued that the Biennial world conference with its call for papers and the co-sponsorship of the journal, International Social Work, are particularly important to the mission of the IASSW as both address the purpose of advancing scholarship and research in social work and social work education.

IASSW played a lead role in the establishment of the journal and guided it in its early years. To further this objective of encouraging scholarship and research, IASSW has recently expanded its publication activity and has launched a book series through Venture Press. IASSW also assisted the Caribbean sub-regional group to launch The Caribbean Journal of Social Work in 2002. In the 1970's IASSW secured significant funding to pursue a 6 year multi-country project on family planning and social work education.

The project was implemented in 20 countries-as diverse as Iran, the Philippines, Kenya, and Jamaica. Curricula, field placements, project reports and a number of important publications resulted from the effort. The family planning project put IASSW on the forefront of a cutting edge issue and reflected sound working relationships with major governmental and private funding bodies. While no initiative of this scale has been implemented since then, IASSW was active in the 1980's and 1990's to promote and assist the development of social work education in Eastern Europe, Russia and China.

Consultations and seminars were sponsored to help countries establish or re-establish social work. Through recent efforts to strengthen the regional association of schools of social work in Africa and assistance in the establishment of sub-regional organisations in the Caribbean in the 1990s and in Southeast Europe in 2006, promotion of the growth and development of social work education continues to be a programme priority of the IASSW. In an effort to promote international exchange and innovation, IASSW began a programme of small projects in 2004. A consortium of at least 3 schools in two or more countries with different cultures or social work educational systems may apply for funding for a project that advances social work education internationally.

The projects must enhance international and cross-cultural collaboration. To date, among the projects that have been funded are one to develop a website on field education for Chinese schools of social work; a collaboration of schools in Kenya, the Philippines and England to develop a module on disaster management; a project sponsored by 18 schools in 9 different countries on indigenous social work education and practice; and a 10 country project on international social work and political conflict resolution that is setting up a network to enhance social work education and research in conflict and post-conflict situations.

IASSW led the effort to develop Global Standards for Social Work Education and Training, adopted by both IFSW and IASSW in 2004. This comprehensive document is the first set of standards for social work education at the global level. Although compliance with the standards is voluntary, they have been hailed by schools of social work-especially in the developing world-as helpful targets that will contribute to upgrading of social work training. IASSW also joined with IFSW in developing and endorsing the Global Definition of Social Work and the Statement of Ethical Principles.

There are two categories of membership in the IASSW: school members and individual members. Social Work educational programmes at the tertiary level are eligible to join as school members. Individual educators may also join, but individual member votes count as 1/10 of a school vote. Currently, there are member schools in more than 70 countries spread across Africa, Asia and the Pacific, Europe, Latin America, and North American and the Caribbean. Schools are also organised into regional associations. Although the regions differ greatly in their degree of formality and organisation, each regional President serves on the IASSW Board and Executive Committee as a Vice-President.

The Board of Directors is large and includes the elected officers of President, Secretary and Treasurer; 4 elected at-large members; regional representatives, including the Vice-Presidents; and national representatives. Chairs of task forces and committees also attend board meetings where they have a voice, but not a vote. Current committees and task forces include the International Exchange Task Force, the Nominating Committee, an award committee, the World Census Committee, the Women's Caucus, Publications, Human Rights, the Projects Committee, and the UN representatives team.

IASSW has faced several challenges over its almost 80 years of existence. Among them were the devastation and disruption caused by World War II and the financial difficulties of the early 1990's that led to the loss of

Secretariat. In the 1980's, the organisation faced a different kind of struggle over the membership of South African schools. The world's attention on the evils of the South African apartheid system intensified during the late 1970's and 1980's. A major initiative was to isolate the South African government by expelling South African organisations from participation in world bodies and events.

The issue extended to social work education. Throughout the 1980's there was extensive work to assess the degree to which the South African schools were working to oppose apartheid and to ensure multiracial social work education. When the IASSW leadership decided to work with the reform-oriented South African schools and allow the JUC to retain membership, the schools in the Nordic region withdrew. Although reconciliation and re-entry of the Nordic schools occurred after the end of apartheid, the struggle over South Africa had a long lasting effect on the organisation.

Future challenges include pressures arising from changes in the educational sector, where mergers of social work programmes into larger departments with other disciplines are becoming more common. When social work has less autonomy and less visibility, there is diminished allegiance to the profession and schools are less likely to maintain membership in social work organisations such as the IASSW. While the Global Standards are a major advance, they are voluntary and some are concerned that free trade regulations will lead to externally-imposed criteria for social work education.

IASSW needs to carefully monitor such developments and be prepared to respond. The process of developing the standards also gave renewed attention to the continuing challenge to achieve some universality-definition of what is essential and core education for professional social work-while encouraging diversity and indigenisation of curricula.

International Council on Social Welfare (ICSW)

The International Council on Social Welfare differs from the IFSW and IASSW because it is interdisciplinary and includes lay as well as professional members. The ICSW is "a global non-governmental organisation which represents a wide range of national and international member organisations that seek to advance social welfare, social justice and social development".

ICSW describes its mission as: "to promote forms of social and economic development which aim to reduce poverty, hardship and vulnerability throughout the world, especially amongst disadvantaged people". The statement continues: "It strives for recognition and protection of fundamental rights to food, shelter, education, health care and security. It believes that these rights are an essential foundation for freedom, justice and peace. It seeks also to advance equality of opportunity, freedom of self-expression and access to human services".

The ICSW, under the earlier name of the International Conference on Social Work, was formed in 1928 out of the Paris conference with Rene Sand, a chief organiser of the 1928 meetings, as its founder and Alice Masarykova as first president. Sand soon succeeded Masarykova as President in 1932. Organised to promote the interests of the social welfare sector and to ensure international exchange of information and views, the ICSW held international conferences in 1932 and 1936, resuming in the post-World War II years.

Records of the planning for a 1940 conference and all records of the early ICSW were destroyed in the bombing of London. Rene Sand's own story illustrates the disruption of organisational activities during the war years. He was taken prisoner in 1940 when the Nazi army invaded Belgium and was held in Tyrol, Austria until he was liberated in May of 1945. He resumed his active presidency of ICSW until 1948 when he encouraged younger leaders to take over.

ICSW regrouped after the war, focusing initially on relief for war-torn areas. A special meeting was held in 1947 in Holland on the theme: "Urgent Social Problems in the War Stricken Areas of Europe". The ICSW was one of the first NGOs to gain consultative status with the United Nations. Conference locations marked progress of the ICSW in the post-war years. The 1952 conference in Madras, India, was the first held outside the West. In 1956, the conference was held in Munich with participants from 55 countries.

As Katzki observed, support for the conference in Germany showed that "participants recognised in ICSW a force that could help heal wounds and contribute to a better understanding amongst peoples". Geographic reach was extended through the 1962 conference in Brazil and the 1974 conference in Nairobi, Kenya. It is worth noting that ICSW gave early recognition to human rights. The 1968 conference theme "Social Welfare and Human Rights" supported the United Nations International Year of Human Rights.

The papers delivered at the conference contain messages relevant to this day. The human rights theme was echoed in 1976 in Puerto Rico: "The Struggle for Equal Opportunity-Strategies for Social Welfare." The organisation sought ways to expand its activities beyond the biennial conferences. In 1966, the name of the organisation was changed to the International Council on Social Welfare to more accurately convey that membership and scope of activity are not limited to social work.

Katzki records that by 1968, ICSW had almost 50 national committees in membership and that many of these were in developing countries. Efforts continued to strengthen national committees and build regional networks. A particularly important area of activity is consultation at the United Nations. ICSW has the highest level of NGO consultative status with the United Nations and relates to the Economic and Social Council (ECOSOC), as well as to the ILO, UNICEF, UNESCO, WHO and other bodies.

The Category I consultative status allows ICSW to attend ECOSOC meetings, circulate written statements to members, address a council committee, and submit items for ECOSOC consideration. For at least 25 years, ICSW has emphasised social development. In 1982, ICSW officially described itself as: International Council on Social Welfare: A World Organisation Promoting Social Development. The emphasis on social development intensified in preparations for and participation in the 1995 United Nations World Summit on Social Development held in Copenhagen.

ICSW participated in the preparatory meetings for the Summit and organised a global NGO preparatory meeting. More than 60 NGO leaders attended this meeting in Helsinki in 1994. Over several years prior to and during the Summit, ICSW distributed copies of its policy papers on poverty and other Summit issues, monitored the official deliberations, and worked collaboratively with other NGOs. The Chair of the ICSW Summit Working Group, Julian Disney, reported success: "ICSW widely circulated about a dozen policy papers and proposals for inclusion in the Summit agreements and we are pleased that many of our recommendations are reflected in the final documents".

After the Summit, the organisation has continued to participate in the activities of the Commission on Social

Development and to monitor progress on the commitments agreed at the Summit. In 1997, ICSW signed a Memorandum of Understanding with UNDP to ensure closer cooperation on matters related to civil society, poverty eradication and social development. ICSW has continued to represent issues of social welfare and social development at numerous international meetings, including the World Economic Forum, the International Labour Conference, WHO, and the UN Commission for Social Development.

More recently, ICSW has been critical of the narrow definition of poverty expressed in the Millennium Development Goals (MDGs) and called for inclusion of the ideas expressed in the Summit Commitments. ICSW identifies employment as an important component of the fight against poverty, yet employment is neglected in the MDGs. The emphasis of the 2007 Social Development Commission UN meeting is on decent work for all, a theme actively supported by the ICSW.

ICSW makes its contribution through research and dissemination of information, exchange through conferences, and development of policy recommendations based on its research and linkages with local and national organisations. ICSW experienced leadership difficulties early in the 21st century, when the elected President was harassed and jailed in his home country of Bangladesh. This coincided with a time when the organisation was also without a permanent Executive Director.

Nonetheless, programmes have continued. Global conferences were held in Malaysia in 2004 and in Brazil in 2006, with more than 1000 participants from 44 countries. A four-year plan for ongoing programmes was adopted in 2004. Regional activities have intensified as ICSW carries out its goal of "strengthening civil society in all parts of the world".

Initiatives included efforts in Central and West Africa and the Black Sea area. In Europe, work at the European Regional Conference emphasised a "European Social Model" to promote balanced social and economic progress, equal rights, and solidarity. A link with the South Asia Partnership has worked on such critical issues as trafficking, democracy and disasters.

There are several different membership categories. National Committees of ICSW are country level bodies that represent non-governmental organisations in the social welfare/social development field. There are currently national committees in 32 countries that are members. In addition, ICSW has International Member Organisations-global and/or regional organisations that support ICSW goals; and a number of members classified as Other Organisations who can affiliate within regions; and finally, Government Associates. There are currently member organisations in at least 50 countries.

The disruption caused by the arrest of the President of the ICSW in 2000 was described above and obviously posed a serious challenge to the organisation. But, the ICSW has recovered and is actively pursuing an ambitious programme. In 2004, ICSW adopted a 4-year global programme with seven areas of work. These are: social welfare and social development; networking; communicating with stakeholders; global advocacy on "socially responsible global governance"; regional co-operation; North-South partnerships; and South-South policy dialogue. A challenge is the lack of strong national committees in some countries.

According to the Executive Director, "the emphasis of ICSW's current global programme is to strengthen national umbrella organisations in the South. This is fundamental to achieving our goal of influencing governments to take seriously the road to reducing poverty in their countries and their regions". While establishing strong and sustainable national civil society organisations in the Global South may be particularly difficult, the problem also exists in industrialised countries. The United States, for example, no longer has a strong national committee and its participation in the ICSW has diminished.

CONFLICT AMONG THE THREE ORGANISATIONS

The three organisations have many common areas of interest and activity. All hold conferences, support the journal International Social Work, maintain consultative status at the UN and aim to represent social work and social welfare at a number of NGO committees and activities. All emphasise the value of international exchange and communication and all have continued to seek ways to strengthen their organisational activities and contributions between and beyond conferences.

IFSW and IASSW have successfully collaborated in and sponsored an annual Social Work Day at the UN in New York. In 2007, a World Social Work Day has been launched by the IFSW and creates additional opportunities for collaborative efforts. At some points in history, there have been conflicts within and between the organisations, especially over the status of apartheid South Africa. At other times, disagreements or barriers to collaboration have been more mundane-disputes over conference locations, expenditures, or hurt feelings over failure to give due credit to contributions of the collaborating partners.

While mundane, these can be difficult to resolve and can pose obstacles to successfully speaking with a unified voice on the international scene. Perhaps more distressing have been the consequences caused when the organisations and their leaders have been persecuted for their advocacy work. Over the course of history, each organisation has suffered. In the 1930's, the President of

IASSW was pressured by her own German colleagues to resign as she was deemed unfit by the Nazis. More recently, the elected President of the ICSW.

Qazi Faruque Ahmed of Bangladesh, was unable to fulfill his duties as he and his local organisation were persecuted by the government of the country. While pressure from ICSW members and others resulted in his release from jail, Dr. Ahmed was unable to serve as President due to this situation. Oppression and conflict have taken their toll many times, including the early 1990's when the head of the IFSW's Kuwait Association of Social Workers was captured and later killed by the Iraqi invaders.

As a profession concerned with social justice and human rights, social work is seen as highly political and therefore as a threat to oppressive governments. This continues to put social work organisations and their leaders in danger. The commonality of goals and programme priorities suggest that the organisations can share successful strategies and lessons learned. All three organisations are working to strengthen the regions, identify and encourage growth of membership in Africa, Asia and Latin America, and promote increased communication and networking. Now that the organisations have agreed to co-host their world conferences, more emphasis on sharing information and successes can begin.

Collaboration is important, but often challenging. IFSW, IASSW and ICSW have agreed that future world conferences will be jointly planned and held. There is a danger that a large and commonly planned conference will result in loss of important elements of each organisation's needs and programme. It is interesting to note that in a 1996 analysis of the contributions of the journal International Social Work, John Lawrence called for ICSW to discontinue its co-sponsorship to allow social work to strengthen and unify its voice.

In a combined effort, care must be taken to ensure that attention to both education and practice is ensured and that participants who are not social workers are not overwhelmed by professional considerations. In spite of dangers, collaboration is more important than ever. There is a compelling need to speak with a unified voice in order to represent social work and social welfare concerns more forcefully on the world scene.

The impacts of neoliberalism and globalisation have only intensified the need for progress on issues of poverty and human rights. For IFSW and IASSW, a future challenge will be to see how with ICSW the organisations can promote social welfare and social development without losing the professional focus, and a key consideration will be to ensure that the definition of social work remains up-todate and relevant to global concerns. It is important for social workers and those devoted to social welfare and social development to remember the enthusiasm of the founders as they succeeded in organising the first world conference and then the new organisations.

Bibliography

Ahmad, B., *Black Perspectives in Social Work,* Birmingham: Venture Press, 1990.

Aldgate, J., 'Evolution not Revolution: Family Support Services and the Children Act 1989.' in Ward, H. and Rose, W. (eds.) *Approaches to Needs Assessment in Children's Services.* London: Jessica Kingsley, 2002.

Aviram, U., 'The Changing Role of the Social Worker in the Mental Health System', *Social Work in Health Care,* 2002.

Baldwin, M., "Care Management and Social Work Theory and Care Managers Assess their own Practice", in Baldwin, M. *Care Management and Community Care: Social Work Discretion and the Construction of Policy,* 2000.

Balloch, S., McLean, J and Fisher, M. (eds.), *Social Services Working Under Pressure,* Bristol: The Policy Press, 1999.

Lavalette, M. and Pratt, A. (eds.), *Social Policy: A Conceptual and Methodological Introduction,* Sage: London, 2004.

Elder-Woodward, J., "Social Work and Disabled People: from crafting clients to sustaining citizens", *Paper given at a day conference,* Scottish Community Development Centre, 2002.

Evans, C. and Carmichael, A., *Users' Best Value: A Guide to User Involvement in Best Practice Reviews,* York: Joseph Rowntree Foundation, 2002.

Gambrill, E., 'The Future of Evidence-based Social Work Practice' in Thyer, B. and Kazi, M. A. F. (eds.), *International Perspectives on Evidence-based Practice in Social Work,* 2004.

Harding, T. and Beresford, P., *The Standards We Expect: what services users and carers want from social services workers,* London: National Institute for Social Work, 1996.

Kearney, P., Levin, E. and Rosen, G., *Alcohol, Drugs and Mental Health Problems: Working with Families*, London: National Institute for Social Work, 2000.

Levin, L. and Moriarty, J., *Research on Community Care: Social Work and Community Care Arrangements for Older People with Dementia*, London: National Institute for Social Work, 1998.

Marsh, P. and Fisher, M., *Good Intentions: Developing Partnerships in Social Services*, York: Joseph Rowntree Foundation, 1992.

Perlman, H. H., "Social work method: A review of the decade. 1955-65", *SocialWork*, 1965.

Skinner, A., "Growth and Development: Social Work Services for the 21st Century", the *Report of the Chief Inspector of Social Work Services for Scotland*, Edinburgh: Scottish Executive, 2002.

Smale, G., Tuson, G. and Statham, D., *Social Work and Social Problems*, London: Macmillan Press, 2000.

Waterhouse, L. and McGhee, J., "Social Work in Scotland After Devolution" in Payne, M. and Shardlow, S. M. (eds.) *Social Work in the British Isles*, London: Jessica Kingsley, 2002.

Index